ENDORSEMENTS FOR

Guided by the Directory for Catechesis

Here at last is an outstanding and easy-to-read short course in contemporary catechesis and faith formation as the Church envisions it! It's powerful, clear, and filled with practical help. I'd like to put this book into the hands of every catechetical leader—including every pastor—in the church! You will read and re-read this, write notes in the margins, and use it to shape how you pass on the faith in your parish.

BILL HUEBSCH *is author of **Promise and Hope: Pastoral Theology in the Age of Mercy** and a long-time catechetical leader*

This powerful companion to the *Directory for Catechesis* offers catechetical leaders a new way forward for adapting catechesis for the ages and stages of life. The authors uniquely apply a synodal process of journeying, listening, and discerning as a community illuminated by the doctrinal wisdom of the *Directory* toward shaping a renewed vision and designing effective practices for lifelong formation in faith.

JAYNE RAGASA-MONDOY *is a catechetical consultant and author of **Cultivating Your Catechists***

Guided by the Directory for Catechesis: Transforming the Vision and Practice of Parish Catechesis is a blueprint for anyone interested in creating meaningful faith formation experiences. Each chapter features insights from the *Directory* along with practical online resources that catechetical leaders can use with their teams to evaluate, vision, and plan. A great resource for parishes who want to develop Christ-centered catechesis for people of all ages!

AMY AUZENNE *is Director of the Office of Evangelization and Catechesis, Archdiocese of Galveston-Houston*

When the *Directory for Catechesis* came out, we enthusiastically promoted it, taught it, and strove to put it in the hands of every catechetical leader. But I fear that, for many busy leaders, it remained on a bookshelf, an untapped resource. But now, *Guided by the Directory for Catechesis* gives parish leaders the practical tools to tap into the vision and principles of the *Directory* and to apply them directly in planning, reviving and reinventing faith formation in their own parish. This is the companion piece that takes the Church's vision off the shelf and puts it where catechetical leaders can make a difference.

GARY POKORNY *is the former Director of Catechesis for the Archdiocese of Milwaukee and Chairperson of the NCCL Board*

Guided by the Directory for Catechesis offers a wonderful opportunity to explore and ponder the question that many fall upon after reading the *Directory for Catechesis*: "so, what?" In guiding readers through an exercise of "developing a shared vison of catechesis" for catechetical ministry in their parish to offering practical steps in implementing the frameworks of the *Directory*, this book not only communicates the richness of catechesis, but also offers a creative religious imagination that will inspire catechists and catechetical ministry teams to engage in new forms of catechesis that respond to the formation needs of the Church of today and tomorrow. The wisdom offered by LaVecchia, Roberto, and Schaeffler, lifelong catechetical ministers, is not to be missed, but relished and shared.

DR. JODI HUNT *is Executive Director of the Neuhoff Institute*
for Ministry and Evangelization at the University of Dallas

This book is a comprehensive analysis that unpacks the *Directory for Catechesis* and offers ideas and strategies to implement it in parish settings to influence effective lifelong catechesis for all ages. It takes the document of the Church and enlivens it with a multitude of relevant questions for reflection and discussion. Because of its digestible, practical, and vibrant presentation it will be useful in ministry and adult formation programs and settings. It is a guidebook for leaders who want to implement innovative catechesis in their parish considering the most current guidance.

DR. KATHIE AMIDEI *is Pastoral Associate at St. Anthony on the Lake Parish in Pewaukee, WI*
*and author of **Learning Together: Forming Faith in Families, An Intergenerational Resource***

Guided by the Directory for Catechesis sets the stage for clergy and lay catechetical leaders to discern and design comprehensive faith formation processes to draw adults, youth, and children closer to Jesus Christ in the Catholic church of the United States. The authors offer vision, best practices, application strategies, practical questions, and resources to lead catechetical teams to imagine and create new models for all to encounter Christ. May the Holy Spirit guide us in this moment of creative grace for catechesis in the context of evangelization.

JOSE AMAYA *is Director of Faith Formation for the Archdiocese of the Military Services*

Clear, faithful, practical, and inspiring, *Guided by the Directory for Catechesis* is a must-have resource for anyone with responsibility for leading parish faith formation. Both the content and the processes echo the principles of kerygmatic, evangelizing catechesis that keep dialogue with Jesus Christ, the Church, and the world at the heart of who we are and how we are called to be in accompanying people to recognize God already present in their real-life circumstances.

DR. LORI DAHLHOFF *is a catechetical consultant and author*
*of **Reflections and Prayers to Nourish New Catholics***

GUIDED *by the* DIRECTORY *for* CATECHESIS

Transforming the Vision and Practice of Parish Catechesis

CATHERINE LAVECCHIA ■ JOHN ROBERTO
JANET SCHAEFFLER, OP

TWENTY-THIRD PUBLICATIONS

twentythirdpublications.com

TWENTY-THIRD PUBLICATIONS

977 Hartford Turnpike Unit A

Waterford, CT 06385

(860) 437-3012 or (800) 321-0411

www.twentythirdpublications.com

IMAGE CREDITS

Cover art: © dmitrydesigner / stock.adobe.com

Interior images: page 45 - Rido / stock.adobe.com; page 54 - Konstantin Yuganov / stock.adobe.com; page 59 - New Africa / stock.adobe.com; page 68 - CarlosBarquero / stock.adobe.com; page 73 - Prostock-studio / stock.adobe.com; page 85 - bnenin / stock.adobe.com

ISBN: 978-1-62785-813-7

Printed in the U.S.A.

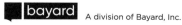 A division of Bayard, Inc.

Contents

A New Moment for Catechesis in the Catholic Church

The title of our book—*Guided by the Directory for Catechesis: Transforming the Vision and Practice of Parish Catechesis*—is also our goal. We are offering this book as a way for your parish to utilize the *Directory* as the guide to developing holistic, effective, innovative, and lifelong catechesis for all ages that speaks to the new context in which we live. We want the *Directory* to come alive in your parish community.

This is the third catechetical directory issued since Vatican II. The 1971 *General Catechetical Directory* presented the first contemporary vision of catechesis in the Catholic Church and affirmed the vision of catechesis that evolved during the modern catechetical movement of the 1950s and 1960s. It emphasized that the aim of catechesis is promoting a maturing of faith throughout life. The GCD presented adult catechesis as the model and norm for all catechesis. The primary arena for catechesis was seen as the community rather than the classroom; and the people (catechists and teachers) who hand on faith were regarded more highly than catechisms (though catechisms still had a place). It described a more comprehensive catechesis that could be systematic or occasional, for individuals or communities, organized or spontaneous.

The 1997 *General Directory for Catechesis* built on over twenty years of development in catechetical thinking and practice. The goal of all catechesis was "communion and intimacy with Jesus Christ"—a living encounter with Jesus Christ. Among the central themes of the GDC were an emphasis on discipleship and continuing conversion; a Church of living signs that is the source, locus, and means of salvation; six interrelated tasks that flow from the ministry of Jesus—knowledge of the faith, liturgical celebration, morality, prayer, community life, and missionary spirit; the catechumenate as a model and inspiration for all catechizing activity; and the church of the home as a unique locale for catechesis.

The 2020 *Directory for Catechesis* builds on the vision of the two earlier documents while speaking directly to the new moment in which we live. In chapter 1, we highlight several features of the *Directory*'s vision:

- Catechesis is accompaniment, education, and formation in the faith and for the faith.

- Catechesis fosters communion and intimacy with Jesus Christ at the center of all catechetical action.

- Catechesis is a living encounter with Jesus Christ that transforms a person's whole life—mind, heart, and body.

- Catechesis is centered on the kerygma—the life, message, death, and resurrection of Jesus—which is the heart of catechesis with all ages.

- Catechesis fosters ongoing maturation in faith.

- Catechesis is pedagogical action at the service of the dialogue of salvation between God and humanity and is inspired by the features of the divine pedagogy: God's gratuitous love, salvation, conversion, the word of God, centrality of Jesus Christ, community experience of faith, and pedagogy of signs.

- Catechesis is carried out in fidelity to the word of God and in attention to and interaction with the educational practices of the culture.

The *Directory for Catechesis* also presents foundational practices to shape catechetical ministry in a parish community. In chapter 2, we highlight eight important catechetical practices in the *Directory*:

1. Catechesis is responsive to the diversity in the religious-spiritual lives of people today, personalizing catechesis to address their spiritual-religious needs and journeys.

2. Catechesis is inspired by the model and process of the baptismal catechumenate—with its stages of growth accommodated to people's journey in faith—providing a way to personalize catechesis around the faith journeys of people from initial proclamation through mystagogy.

3. Catechesis incorporates three faith-forming environments at every stage of life to foster growth in faith: intergenerational community, three-generational family, and age groups.

4. Catechesis speaks to the needs, traditions, and spirituality of each culture in the parish and implements approaches to address the uniqueness of each culture.

5. Catechesis builds a culture of full inclusion in the life of the Church and all catechetical programming for persons with disabilities, utilizing educational methods that meet the needs of children and young people with disabilities.

6. Catechesis views human experience as integral to catechesis—in its identity and process, in its content and methods—as it seeks to help illuminate and interpret people's experiences of life in the light of the Gospel.

7. Catechesis utilizes a variety of processes and methods for educating and forming people in the faith and for the faith in ways that are appropriate to the age and intellectual development of people.

8. Catechesis in a digital culture utilizes a variety of digital tools and approaches, including online learning and hybrid models of learning that integrate online and face-to-face learning in physical settings.

We believe the *Directory for Catechesis* can transform the vision and practices of catechesis in every parish community. We have designed this book as a practical manual to help you apply the *Directory* to your setting. The flow of the book leads you *from vision to practices to application to design*. Be sure to have a copy of the *Directory for Catechesis* by your side as you make the journey from vision to design.

The Flow of the Book

CHAPTER 1: Fashioning a Catechetical Vision for the Parish is designed to help your parish develop a shared vision for catechesis informed by the *Directory for Catechesis* that brings clarity to your parish's catechetical ministry. Chapter 1 also guides you in developing goals for lifelong maturing in faith that can inform the design of catechetical ministry with families and all ages. We are strong believers in moving away from a program-centered catechesis to a vision- and goal-centered catechesis.

CHAPTER 2: Shaping the Catechetical Practices of the Parish presents eight principles and practices, informed by the *Directory*, to shape the practice of catechetical ministry in your parish. We provide application activities for each of the eight practices so you can envision how the *Directory* can transform your catechetical ministry.

CHAPTER 3: Designing Catechesis for Families presents insights from the *Directory*'s vision of catechesis *in* the family—focusing on parents nurturing faith; *with* the family—focusing on the parish community forming the faith of families; and *of* the family—focusing on the family proclaiming the Gospel. The chapter includes practical strategies for designing new initiatives in parent and family faith formation.

CHAPTER 4: Designing Catechesis for Children presents insights from the *Directory*'s vision of catechesis with young children (ages 0–5) and grade-school children (ages 6–10) and offers practical strategies for designing new initiatives in children's catechesis that flow from the *Directory*'s practices.

CHAPTER 5: Designing Catechesis for Adolescents presents insights from the *Directory*'s vision of catechesis with pre-adolescents (ages 10–14) and young people/older adolescents/young adults (ages 14–21) and offers practical strategies for designing new initiatives in adolescent catechesis that flow from the *Directory*'s practices.

CHAPTER 6: Designing Catechesis for Adults presents insights from the *Directory*'s vision of catechesis with adults and the elderly and offers practical strategies for designing new initiatives in adult catechesis that flow from the *Directory*'s practices.

CHAPTER 7: Designing Catechesis for the Whole Community Together presents five strategies for engaging the whole community intergenerationally in catechesis.

CHAPTER 8: Designing New Catechetical Initiatives in the Parish guides you through a process to create new initiatives in parish catechesis: empathize with your audience, define the challenge, connect to the *Directory*, generate ideas and strategies, create new initiatives, test, and evaluate.

In each chapter, we include a link to reproducible Practice Resources that you can download for free from the NCCL website at **ncclcatholic.org/guided-by-the-directory**.

We believe that catechesis can form, renew, and revitalize the faith life of the whole parish community. It can contribute toward building a thriving parish community that becomes a learning community that lives its mission in the world. How and what a parish community is learning is essential to building a vital parish community.

When a parish embraces lifelong formation in faith as essential to its mission and makes a commitment to create and sustain catechesis with families and all ages, the culture of the Church is strengthened and the faith of individuals flourishes.

We believe that implementing the vision and practices in the *Directory for Catechesis* can lead your parish community toward thriving and flourishing.

Fashioning a Catechetical Vision for the Parish

Catechesis makes the proclamation of the passion, death and resurrection of Jesus Christ continually resound in the heart of every person, so that life may be transformed. A dynamic and complex reality at the service of the Word of God, catechesis is accompaniment, education, and formation in the faith and for the faith, an introduction to the celebration of the Mystery, illumination and interpretation of human life and history. By harmoniously integrating these characteristics, catechesis expresses the richness of its essence and offers its specific contribution to the pastoral mission of the Church. (*DIRECTORY FOR CATECHESIS*, 55)

The Purpose of Catechetical Ministry

Take a moment to ask yourself: *Why does our parish have a catechetical ministry? Is there a vision and purpose for catechesis in our parish? Is it clear what we are trying to accomplish in the lives of all ages and generations in our community through catechetical ministry?*

If you were to ask parish leaders and members of your community, what would they say is the "why" of catechetical ministry—its purpose? How would they answer the question *What are we trying to accomplish in the lives of people of all ages and generations through the parish's catechetical ministry?*

These questions go to the heart of the "why" of catechetical ministry. Why is catechesis one of the primary and essential ministries of the Church?

The *Directory for Catechesis* addresses this question, providing the meaning, purpose, and vision for catechesis with all ages and generations.

The "why" of catechetical ministry—the vision—leads to "how we do catechetical ministry"—the practices—and is completed by "what we do"—the activities we conduct to bring the vision and practices alive in our parishes. The "why" gives purpose, meaning, and direction to the "how" and the "what."

A shared vision of catechesis in the parish makes explicit what catechesis is, what the parish is trying to achieve, and why it matters! It provides direction and focus. It inspires and motivates leaders and the community. It makes clear the ends toward which you are working. It guides planning and decision-making, ensuring alignment between vision, practices, and activities. It provides a way to measure effectiveness and drive continuous improvement.

APPLICATION

Every parish has a catechetical vision. It may be expressed or not. It may guide everything you do or not. Even if you think your parish does not have a vision, there are assumptions that guide what your parish is doing.

Let's begin with the vision already present in your parish community. Begin with your own personal reflection. If you have a catechetical team, do this as a team exercise. You may even want to interview parish leaders to get their input. Reflect on these two questions to begin:

- Why does our parish have a catechetical ministry?

- What is the purpose of catechetical ministry in our parish?

Develop a series of statements that capture the parish's purpose for catechetical ministry.

We believe the purpose of catechesis in our parish is to...

Insights from the *Directory for Catechesis*

The *Directory for Catechesis* presents the Church's vision and practices for catechesis today and serves as a guide for the development of your parish's vision of catechesis. The following summary statements and quotes from the *Directory* describe the nature and identity of catechesis within the evangelizing mission of the Church. Discern how the *Directory's* vision can be incorporated into your parish's vision.

1 Catechesis is accompaniment, education, and formation in the faith and for the faith.

Catechesis is an ecclesial act, arising from the missionary mandate of the Lord (cf. Matt 28:19–20) and aimed, as its very nature indicates, at making the proclamation of his passion, death and resurrection of Jesus Christ continually resound in the heart of every person, so that life may be transformed. A dynamic and complex reality at the service of the Word of God, catechesis is accompaniment, education, and formation in the faith and for the faith, an introduction to the celebration of the Mystery, illumination and interpretation of human life and history. (55)

Catechesis, a privileged stage in the process of evangelization, is generally directed toward persons who have already received the first proclamation, within whom it promotes the processes of initiation, growth, and maturation in faith. (56)

2 Communion with Jesus Christ is the center of catechetical action.

Communion with Jesus Christ is the center of catechetical action. Catechesis promotes a living encounter with Christ—mind, heart, and body—forming people in getting to know Jesus Christ and his Gospel of liberating salvation, choosing Jesus' way of life, and living the mission of Christ in the world today.

At the center of every process of catechesis is the living encounter with Christ. "Accordingly the definitive aim of catechesis is to put people not only in touch but in communion, in intimacy, with Jesus Christ: only he can lead us to the love of the Father in the Spirit and make us share in the life of the Holy Trinity (CT5)." Communion with Christ is the center of the Christian life, and as a result the center of catechetical action. Catechesis is oriented toward forming persons who get to know Jesus Christ and his Gospel of liberating salvation ever better; who live a profound encounter with him and who choose his own way of life and his very sentiments (cf. Phil 2:5), striving to realize, in the historical situations in which they live, the mission of Christ, which is the proclamation of the kingdom of God. (75)

3 Catechesis is a living encounter with Jesus Christ that transforms a person's whole life—mind, heart, and body.

Catechesis proclaims the Good News of Jesus and his saving death and resurrection so people may be transformed into disciples of Jesus Christ. Catechesis forms families and people of all ages in getting to know Jesus Christ and his Gospel of liberating salvation, choosing Jesus' way of life, and living the mission of Christ in the world today.

A robust and vital Christian faith is a way of the head, the heart, and the hands—informing, forming, and transforming people in Christian faith and identity. "'You shall love the Lord your God with all your heart, and with all your soul, and with all your mind.' This is the greatest and first commandment. And a second is like it: 'You shall love your neighbor as yourself'" (Matt 22:37–39).

The encounter with Christ involves the person in his(her) totality: heart, mind, senses. It does not concern only the mind, but also the body and above all the heart. In this sense catechesis, which helps in the internationalization of the faith and thereby makes an irreplaceable contribution to the encounter with Christ, is not alone in foster-

ing the pursuit of this goal. It is joined in this by the other dimensions of the life of faith: in liturgical-sacramental experience, in affective relationships, in community life and the service of one's brothers(sisters).... (76)

Catechesis makes the initial conversion ripen and helps Christians to give a complete meaning to their existence, educating them in the *mentality of faith* in keeping with the Gospel, to the point of gradually coming to feel, think, and act like Christ. (77)

4 Catechesis is centered in the kerygma— the life, message, death, and resurrection of Jesus—which is the heart of catechesis with all ages and generations.

People hear the proclamation of the Good News of Jesus and his saving death and resurrection so they may be transformed into disciples of Jesus Christ. (See *Directory for Catechesis*, 57–60.)

Kerygmatic catechesis, which goes to the very heart of the faith and grasps the essence of the Christian message, is a catechesis which manifests the action of the Holy Spirit, who communicates God's saving love in Jesus Christ and continues to give himself so that every human being may have the fulness of life. The different formulations of the kerygma, which necessarily open pathways of discovery, correspond to the existential doorways into the mystery. (2)

...Catechesis, which cannot always be distinguished from the first proclamation, is called to be in the first place a proclamation of the faith.... The proclamation can therefore no longer be considered simply the first stage of faith, preliminary to catechesis, but rather the essential dimension of every moment of catechesis. (57)

5 Catechesis fosters ongoing maturation in faith.

The close connection between evangelization and catechesis is one of the distinctive features of the *Directory*. It describes the relationship between the announcement of the *kerygma* (evangelization) and *mystagogy*—its maturation.

> Catechesis participates according to its own nature in the effort of evangelization, in order that the faith may be supported by an ongoing maturation and express itself in a way that must characterize the very being of the disciple of Christ. Because of this, catechesis is related to the liturgy and to charity in making evident the essential unity of the new life which springs forth from Baptism. (1)
>
> Catechesis makes the initial conversion ripen and helps Christians to give a complete meaning to their existence, educating them in a *mentality of faith* in keeping with the Gospel, to the point of gradually coming to feel, think, and act like Christ. (77)
>
> *Catechesis as mystagogic initiation* introduces the believer into the living experience of the Christian community, the true setting of the life of faith. This formation experience is progressive and dynamic; rich in signs and expressions and beneficial for the integration of every dimension of the person. (2)

6 Catechesis is pedagogical action at the service of the dialogue of salvation between God and humanity and is inspired by the features of the divine pedagogy: God's gratuitous love, salvation, conversion, the word of God, centrality of Jesus Christ, community experience of faith, and pedagogy of signs.

> Catechesis is inspired by the features of the divine pedagogy. In this way, it becomes pedagogical action at the service of the dialogue of salvation between God and humanity. It is therefore important that it express the following characteristics:
>
> - making present the initiative of God's gratuitous love;
> - bringing into focus the universal destination of salvation;
> - evoking the conversion necessary for the obedience of faith;
> - adopting the principle of the progressive nature of Revelation and the transcendence of the Word of God, as also its inculturation in human cultures;
> - recognize the centrality of Jesus Christ, the Word of God made man, which establishes catechesis as *pedagogy of the incarnation*;
> - valuing community experience of the faith, as proper to the people of God;
> - putting together a pedagogy of signs, where actions and words are in mutual relationship;
> - recalling that God's inexhaustible love is the ultimate reason for all things. (165)

The way of God who reveals himself and saves, together with the Church's response of faith in history, becomes the source and model for the pedagogy of faith. Catechesis thus presents itself as a process that allows the maturation of the faith through respect for the journey of each individual believer. Catechesis is therefore the *pedagogy of faith in action*, together with *initiation, education*, and *teaching*, always having clear the unity between content and the way it is transmitted.... (166)

7 Catechesis is carried out in fidelity to the word of God and in attention to and interaction with the educational practices of the culture.

In the face of current challenges, it is ever more important to be aware of the reciprocity between content and method, as much in catechesis as in evangelization.... In the journey of catechesis, the principle of *evangelizing by educating* and *educating by evangelizing* recalls among other things, that the work of the catechists consists in finding and drawing attention to the signs of God's action already present in the lives of persons and, by using these as an example, present the Gospel as a transformative power for the whole of existence, to which it will give full meaning. The accompaniment of a person on a journey of growth and conversion is necessarily marked by gradualness, in that the act of believing implies a progressive discovery of the mystery of God and an openness and entrustment to him that grows over time. (179)

Catechesis is an essentially educational action. It is always carried out in fidelity to the word of God and in attention to and interaction with the educational practices of the culture. Thanks to the research and reflections of the human sciences there have arisen theories, approaches, and models that profoundly renew educational practices and make a significant contribution to an in-depth understanding of people, human relationships, society, and history. Their contribution is indispensable. Pedagogy and didactics in particular enrich the educational process of catechesis. Together with them, psychology also has an important value, above all because it helps one to grasp the motivation dynamics, the structure of the personality, the elements relating to problems and pathologies, the different stages of development and developmental tasks, the dynamism of religious maturation, and the experiences that open human beings to the mystery of the sacred. (180)

APPLICATION

Review your purpose statements from the opening reflection. Compare and contrast your parish vision with the seven summary descriptions of the *Directory*'s vision for catechesis. Use the following questions to guide your review and then write a second version of your parish's purpose statements inspired by the *Directory for Catechesis*.

- How does the *Directory* affirm our vision and purpose?

- How does the *Directory* challenge our vision and purpose?

- What do we need to add, revise, or eliminate in our vision?

- How can we enhance our vision and purpose with the *Directory*'s vision?

- How can we expand our vision and purpose with the *Directory*'s vision?

Use the following sentence to develop your second version.

We believe the purpose of catechesis in our parish is to…

Goals for Maturing in Faith

The purpose statements are the first element of fashioning a vision of catechesis for your parish. The second element focuses on your vision of maturing in faith throughout life. Catechesis "promotes the processes of initiation, growth, and maturation in faith" (56). Every parish can benefit from developing shared goals for maturing in the Catholic faith. Catechesis at each stage of life would be guided by one vision of faith maturing expressed through specific goals and life stage–appropriate faith formation.

The *Directory for Catechesis*, like the 1997 *General Directory for Catechesis*, proposes tasks for catechesis that promote an integral Christian life and a holistic formation in faith: 1) knowledge of the faith, 2) understanding and experience of liturgical celebrations, 3) Christian formation of the moral conscience, 4) educating for prayer and in prayer, and 5) developing belonging to the Church and living its mission. These five tasks provide the framework for developing goals for maturing in faith for a lifetime.

The five tasks are inspired by the way Jesus formed his disciples:

In order to achieve its goals, catechesis pursues several interconnected tasks that are inspired by the way in which Jesus formed his disciples: he got them to *know* the mysteries of the Kingdom, taught them to *pray*, proposed to them *gospel values*, initiated them in the life of *communion* with him and among themselves, and into *mission*. The pedagogy of Jesus then molded the life of the Christian community: "they devoted themselves to the apostles' teaching and fellowship, to the breaking of the bread and the prayers" (Acts 2:42). The faith, in fact, demands to be known, celebrated, lived, and turned into prayer. In order to form believers for an integral Christian life catechesis therefore pursues the following tasks: leading to the knowledge of the faith, initiating into the celebration of the mystery, forming for life in Christ, teaching to pray, and introducing to community life. (79)

A holistic formation in faith—at every stage in life—includes five essential and interrelated elements:

LEADING TO THE KNOWLEDGE OF THE FAITH

Catechesis has the task of fostering the knowledge and exploration of the Christian message. In this way it helps the believer to know the truths of the Christian faith, introduces him(her) to the knowledge of Sacred Scripture and of the Church's living Tradition, fosters knowledge of the Creed and the creation of a coherent doctrinal vision that can be used as a reference in life. (80)

INITIATING INTO THE CELEBRATION OF THE MYSTERY

Catechesis…has the task of assisting in the comprehension and experience of liturgical celebrations. Through this task, catechesis helps the believer to understand the importance of liturgy in the Church's life, initiates him(her) into the knowledge of the sacraments and into the sacramental life, especially the sacraments of Eucharist, source and summit of the life and mission of the Church. (81)

FORMING FOR LIFE IN CHRIST

Catechesis has the task of making the heart of every Christian resound with the call to live a new life in keeping with the dignity of children of God received in Baptism and with the life of the Risen One that is communicated through the sacraments...catechesis instructs the believer in following the Lord according to the dispositions described in the Beatitudes.... (83)

...the catechetical task of educating the believer to the good life of the Gospel involves the Christian formation of the moral conscience....This is why it is important to teach the believer to draw from the commandment of charity developed from the Decalogue, and from the virtues, both human and Christian, guidelines for acting as Christians in the different arenas of life. (84)

TEACHING PRAYER

Catechesis has the task of educating the believer for prayer and in prayer, developing the contemplative dimensions of Christian experience. It is necessary to teach him(her) to pray *with* Jesus Christ and *like* him...(86)

The task implies the teaching of both personal prayer and liturgical and community prayer, initiating the believer into the *permanent forms of prayer*: blessing and adoration, petition, intercession, thanksgiving, and praise.... (87)

INTRODUCTION TO COMMUNITY LIFE

The faith is professed, celebrated, expressed, and lived above all in community.... (88)

Catechesis, in reference to preparation for community life, therefore, has the task of developing the sense of belonging to the Church; teaching the sense of ecclesial *communion*, promoting the acceptance of the Magisterium, communion with pastors, fraternal dialogue; forming believers in the sense of ecclesial *co-responsibility*, contributing as active participants to building up

the community and as missional disciples to its growth. (89)

Using the five tasks of catechesis, your parish can develop goals for maturing in faith that apply to all ages throughout life. All catechetical activity can be developed around the goals for maturing in faith through developmentally appropriate experiences, programs, activities, and resources for families and each stage of life: children, adolescents, young adults (20s–30s), midlife adults (40s–50s), mature adults (60s–70s), and older adults (80+).

The goals provide a seamless process of fostering faith growth from birth through older adulthood because everyone shares a common vision of maturing in faith. Individuals, families, and the parish community can visualize how faith can mature from childhood through older adulthood. Catechetical curriculum and programming for families and for all ages and stages of life incorporate and integrate five tasks with their goals to provide a holistic formation in faith and the Christian life.

Here is an example of creating goals for maturing in faith that apply to each stage of life utilizing the holistic formation of the five tasks of catechesis.

Knowledge of the Faith: Fostering knowledge of and exploration of the Christian message in Scripture and the Church's tradition.

Through our parish's catechetical ministry, people of all ages are:

- Learning to live as disciples of Jesus Christ by exploring the kerygma—the life, message, death, and resurrection of Jesus—in the Gospels.

- Reading and studying the Bible and applying its message and meaning to their lives today.

- Learning the Catholic tradition and the foundational teachings of the Catholic faith, and integrating its meaning into their lives as Catholics.

Initiating into the Celebration of the Mystery: Assisting in the comprehension and experience of liturgical celebrations: the sacraments, especially Eucharist, and the feasts and seasons of the liturgical year.

Through our parish's catechetical ministry, people of all ages are:

- Appreciating the significance of the Mass and worshipping God with the community at Sunday Mass.

- Learning the theology and rituals of the Catholic sacraments and celebrating the sacraments throughout life.

- Celebrating and living the seasons of the Church year in their daily lives and with the community.

Forming for Life in Christ: Educating the believer to the good life of the Gospel through the Christian formation of the moral conscience.

Through our parish's catechetical ministry, people of all ages are:

- Learning and internalizing the ethical teachings of the Church and integrating them into decision-making and actions in everyday life.

- Living with moral integrity guided by Catholic moral values.

- Learning Catholic social teaching and living the Church's mission in the world by serving those in need, caring for God's creation, and acting and advocating for justice and peace—locally and globally.

Teaching Prayer: Educating the believer for prayer and in prayer, developing the contemplative dimensions of Christian experience; teaching personal prayer and liturgical and community prayer.

Through our parish's catechetical ministry, people of all ages are:

- Learning to develop a life of prayer that nurtures their relationship with God.

- Growing in a life of prayer through spiritual practices and disciplines.

- Exploring various forms of Catholic spirituality that deepen one's relationship with God.

Introduction to Community Life: Developing the sense of belonging to the Church and contributing as active participants to building up the community and as missional disciples to its growth.

Through our parish's catechetical ministry, people of all ages are:

- Developing a sense of belonging to the Catholic community and participating actively in the life and ministries of the parish community.

- Being equipped to practice their faith in Jesus Christ by using their gifts and talents within the Church and in the world.

Focusing on the five tasks and their goals opens multiple ways (activities, methods, programs) to promote faith and discipleship through developmentally appropriate faith-forming experiences at each stage of life. We build faith formation around the maturing-in-faith goals and then create and curate programs, activities, and resources that are needed to foster faith growth. It moves a parish away from a program-centered catechesis to a goal-centered catechesis with many ways to mature in faith.

With a lifelong vision of maturing faith, a parish can direct energy and attention to specific goals or outcomes in faith maturing. They provide a way to develop a seamless process of fostering faith growth from birth through older adulthood. Everything is in service to people growing in faith and discipleship.

CHAPTER 1
PRACTICE RESOURCES

You will find the following Practice Resource at **ncclcatholic.org/ guided-by-the-directory**:

PRACTICE RESOURCE #1
A Guide to Creating the Purpose and Goals for Catechesis

The *Directory for Catechesis* provides practices to shape catechetical ministry in your parish with all ages and generations.

Shaping the Catechetical Practices of the Parish

The new *Directory for Catechesis* offers fundamental theological-pastoral principles and some general guidelines that are relevant to the practice of catechesis in our time. It is natural that their application and the operative guidelines should be a task for the particular Churches, called to provide an elaboration of these common principles so that they may be inculturated in their own ecclesial context. (*Directory for Catechesis*, 10)

The *Directory for Catechesis* provides practices to shape catechetical ministry in your parish with all ages and generations. This chapter presents eight practices from the *Directory* with ideas for application in parish catechesis.

1. Catechesis with all ages and generations is responsive to the diversity in the religious-spiritual lives of people today, personalizing catechesis to address their spiritual-religious needs and journeys.

2. Catechesis is inspired by the model and process of the baptismal catechumenate—with its stages of growth accommodated to people's journey in faith—providing a way to personalize catechesis around the faith journeys of people from initial proclamation through mystagogy.

3. Catechesis incorporates three faith-forming environments in formation at every stage of life to foster growth in faith: intergenerational community, three-generational family, and age groups.

4. Catechesis speaks to the needs, traditions, and spirituality of each culture in the parish and designs approaches to address the uniqueness of each culture.

5. Catechesis builds a culture of full inclusion in the life of the Church and all catechetical programming for persons with disabilities, utilizing educational methods that meet the needs of children and young people with disabilities.

6. Catechesis views human experience as integral to catechesis—in its identity and process, in its content and methods—as

it seeks to help illuminate and interpret people's experiences of life in the light of the Gospel.

7. Catechesis utilizes a variety of processes and methods for educating and forming people in the faith and for the faith in ways that are appropriate to the age and intellectual development of people.

8. Catechesis in a digital culture utilizes a variety of digital tools and approaches, including online learning and hybrid models of learning that integrate online and face-to-face learning in physical settings.

1 Catechesis with all ages and generations is responsive to the diversity in the religious-spiritual lives of people today, personalizing catechesis to address their spiritual-religious needs and journeys.

We know from research and experience that there is a great diversity in people's religious and spiritual life. The *Directory for Catechesis* describes the diversity in the faith life of adults, a typology that can be applied to ages.

The relationship of adults with the question of faith is highly varied, and it is right that every person should be welcome and listened to in his(her) uniqueness. Without diminishing the uniqueness of each situation, it is possible to consider a few types of adults who live out the faith with different approaches:

- believing adults, who live their faith and want to get to know it better

- adults who, although they may have been baptized, have not been adequately formed or have not brought

Christian initiation to completion, and can be referred to as *quasi-catechumens*

- baptized adults, who although they do not live out their faith on a regular basis, nonetheless seek out contact with the ecclesial community or particular times in life

- adults who come from other Christian confessions or from other religious experiences

- adults who return to the Catholic faith having had experiences in the new religious movements

- unbaptized adults who are candidates for the catechumenate properly so called (258)

One way to envision this diversity is through a continuum of faith and practice—from actively engaged to unaffiliated:

1. People who have a vibrant faith and relationship with God and are engaged in a faith community.

2. People who participate occasionally in the faith community and whose faith is less central to their daily lives.

3. People who are uninvolved in a faith community and who value and live their spirituality outside of organized religion.

4. People who are unaffiliated, have left involvement in organized religion, and have little need for God or religion.

We can see three and even four of these religious profiles reflected in people's participation in church life and catechetical programming. Parents who bring their children for baptism can reflect the whole spectrum, from parents with a vibrant faith to parents who are unaffiliated but whose parents and grandparents are active in a faith community. Children participating in Vacation Bible School may come from families who can reflect all four of these profiles, as do adolescents participating in a confirmation program.

Personalizing catechesis is a way to differentiate catechetical content and methods to address the needs of people in the four types of faith and practice. It moves from a one-size-fits-all style of catechesis to one that is personalized to where people are in their faith journeys. Personalizing faith formation addresses people's diverse faith growth needs by tailoring the faith-forming environment—what, when, how, and where people learn and grow—to address the spiritual and religious interests and needs of families and all ages. It enables faith formation to be individualized and differentiated. Personalization asks, "What is best for you at this time in your life and faith journey?"

The *Directory* recognizes two different types of catechesis—kerygmatic and mystagogic—that are needed to respond to the diversity in religious faith and practice today among all ages and generations. *Kerygmatic catechesis* is focused on the essence of the Christian message—the life, teachings, death, and resurrection of Jesus. *Catechesis as mystagogy* is focused on maturing the faith of the person.

APPLICATION

How could your parish design catechesis with families and each age group and generation that addresses the diverse styles of faith and practice with catechetical experiences, programs, and activities personalized to people's faith journey?

- What would it be like to guide parents, families, young people, and adults in discerning where they are in their faith journey, help them chart a path for faith growth, and provide catechetical experiences, programs, activities, and resources tailored to their religious needs?

- What would it be like to offer catechetical experiences for those who need "taste and see" experiences, "refresher" experiences, "growing" experiences, and "going deeper" experiences?

2 Catechesis is inspired by the model and process of the baptismal catechumenate—with its stages of growth accommodated to people's journey in faith—providing a way to personalize catechesis around the faith journeys of people from initial proclamation through mystagogy.

The *Directory for Catechesis*, like its predecessor the 1997 *General Directory for Catechesis*, advocates for the baptismal catechumenate as the model and process for catechesis with all ages and generations.

Utilizing the catechumenate means "taking on its style and formative dynamism" (64), characterized as Paschal; initiatory; liturgical, ritual, and symbolic; communal; and marked by ongoing conversion and witness and the progress of a formative experience of faith.

- *The Paschal character*: Catechesis communicates the heart of the faith in an essential and existentially understandable way.

- *The initiatory character*: Catechesis provides an introduction to all the dimensions of the Christian life, helping people initiate, with the community, their own personal journey to God.

- *The liturgical, ritual, and symbolic character*: Catechesis, through symbols, rites, and celebrations, can respond to contemporary people, who typically see as significant only those experiences which touch their physical and emotional being.

- *The community character*: Catechesis inspired by the catechumenate integrates the contribution of charisms and ministries of the whole community.

- *The character of ongoing conversion and of witness*: Catechesis is imagined as a journey of conversion that lasts a whole lifetime.

- *The progressive character of the formative experience*: Catechesis is a dynamic process of people growing and maturing over time at their own pace. (Summarized from paragraph 64)

The catechumenal model of formation embodies all five interrelated tasks of catechesis: knowledge of the faith, understanding and experience of liturgical celebrations, Christian formation of the moral conscience, educating for prayer and in prayer, and developing belonging to the Church and living its mission. It is a holistic formation process that includes:

- A first proclamation of the Gospel (kerygma)

- A comprehensive introduction to the Christian life

- Liturgies, rituals, and symbols that engage the heart and the senses

- A community of faith and support

- Apprenticeship and mentoring in faith

- Engagement in the mission of the Church and service to the world

- Formation that fosters conversion of heart and mind in a new way of life

- Ever-deeper formation in faith and the life of the community (mystagogy)

It is an evangelizing catechesis—integrating information, formation, and transformation. It is an apprenticeship in the Christian life. The catechumenal model respects and supports the faith journeys of each individual in a gradual process of formation and transformation.

A parish can embrace the baptismal catechumenate by utilizing the journey of faith in the catechumenal process to develop holistic models of formation for all ages, with special attention to preparation for the sacraments of Marriage, Baptism, First Eucharist, and Confirmation. (See examples of the catechumenal process in the chapters on family, children, adolescents, and adults.)

APPLICATION

How could your parish redesign preparation for Infant Baptism and First Eucharist to reflect the catechumenal model and process?

- What would it be like if your parish personalized parent preparation to address parents (and children) who need a first proclamation of the Gospel (or a refresher) or who need an introduction to the Christian life or need to deepen their faith and practice?

- What would mystagogy look like that accompanies parents and the child in continued faith growth after the sacramental celebration?

How could you redesign Confirmation preparation to reflect the catechumenal model and process?

- What would it be like to personalize the preparation for young people to address the different styles of faith and practice among young people: *active believers* growing in faith and practice, *believers* who are only occasionally involved in the faith community, *inactive believers* who are more spiritual than religious, and *nonbelievers*?

Guided by the Directory for Catechesis

3 Catechesis incorporates three faith-forming environments in formation at every stage of life to foster growth in faith: intergenerational community, three-generational family, and age groups.

At every stage of life, individuals and families need faith-forming experiences through three interconnected environments: the intergenerational parish community; the three-generational family (grandparents, parents, children); and peer groups (or age groups). Research on faith transmission and forming faith reinforce the view that these three interconnected environments provide the best context for catechesis and faith formation across the life span.

Whole Community Intergenerational Catechesis

The Christian community is a primary agent of catechesis. "The faith is professed, celebrated, expressed, and lived above all in community: The communitarian dimension is not just a 'frame,' an 'outline,' but an integral part of the Christian life, of witness and of evangelization" (88).

The *Directory for Catechesis* presents the Christian community, the parish, as "the origin, locus, and goal of catechesis. Proclamation of the Gospel always begins with the Christian community and invites people to conversion and the following of Christ. It is the same community that welcomes those who wish to know the Lord better and permeate themselves with a new life" (133).

Catechesis with the whole community—intergenerational catechesis—engages all ages and generations and is situated within the life of the community.

Intergenerational catechesis envisions the journey of faith as a formative experience not aimed at a particular age group but shared among different generations within a family or a community, on the pathway marked out by the liturgical year. This initiative makes the most of the exchange of the experience of faith among the generations, taking inspiration from the first Christian communities. (232)

Intergenerational catechesis helps parishes live the insight that the community is a primary agent of catechesis where faith is professed, celebrated, expressed, and lived with all ages and generations. Intergenerational catechesis models, approaches, and activities provide the parish with a way to engage all ages and generations together in learning, praying, serving, celebrating, and caring for each other.

An intergenerational church culture forms and deepens Catholic identity and commitment as people develop relationships and actively participate in faith communities that teach, model, and live a distinctive way of life.

APPLICATION: INTERGENERATIONAL

What are the events of community life that can form the basis for intergenerational faith-forming experiences for all ages together? For example:

- The feasts and seasons of the Church year
- Sunday worship and the Lectionary readings
- Rituals and sacramental celebrations
- Acts of service and justice— locally and globally
- Prayer and spiritual traditions
- Contemporary events in the lives of families, the community, and the world

And more

How can catechesis immerse people of all ages more deeply into the experiences of the whole community and help them prepare for and reflect upon their experiences?

 See chapter 7 for intergenerational catechesis strategies.

Family Catechesis

"The family is a community of love and of life, made up of a complex of interpersonal relationships... through which each human person is introduced into the human family and into the family of God which is the Church" (226). A family is the first community and the most basic way in which God gathers us, forms us, and acts in the world.

The family is the primary mechanism by which a Catholic identity becomes rooted in the lives of young people through the day-to-day religious practices and the ways parents model their faith and share with their children. The crucial location where young people's religious outcomes are largely decided is the home; and the primary responsibility for passing on religious faith and practice to children rests with parents. To hand on faith to the next generation, parents must practice their own personal religious faith and serve as role models for their children. Over time, children will learn, absorb, and embrace their own version of the faith.

The family is the primary community where Christian faith practices are nurtured and practiced. Research studies have identified certain faith practices that make a significant difference in nurturing the faith of children and adolescents at home. Raising religious children is primarily a practice-centered process. Among the most important practices are:

- Reading the Bible as a family and encouraging young people to read the Bible regularly

- Praying together as a family and encouraging young people to pray personally

- Serving people in need as a family and supporting service activities by young people

- Eating together as a family

- Having family conversations about faith

- Talking about faith, religious issues, and questions and doubts

- Ritualizing important family moments and milestone experiences

- Celebrating holidays and Church year seasons at home

- Celebrating milestones and sacraments in the lives of individuals and the whole family

- Providing moral instruction

- Being involved in the parish community and participating regularly in Sunday Mass as a family

The *Directory* presents family catechesis in three ways: catechesis *in* the family—emphasizing the role of the family in nurturing faith; catechesis *with* the family—emphasizing the role of the parish community in forming the faith of families centered on the kerygma; and catechesis *of* the family—emphasizing the role of the family in proclaiming the Gospel. These three ways can form the foundation and framework for family catechesis in parish communities.

APPLICATION: FAMILY

How can the parish develop initiatives for catechesis *in* the family which emphasizes the central role of the family in nurturing faith?

- What would it be like to equip parents to incorporate family practices into the ordinary and extraordinary events of family life at home?

- What would it be like to encourage parents to grow in faith and become faith formers of their children?

How can the parish develop initiatives for catechesis *with* the family which emphasizes the role of the parish community in forming the faith of families?

- What would it be like to partner with parents and the whole family in education and formation programming that effectively enhances faith transmission?

- What would it be like to offer family catechesis as a primary model of formation for parents and children and/or to design family-centered sacrament preparation and/or to offer regular family workshops, family festivals, and parent education programming?

How can the parish develop initiatives for catechesis *of* the family which emphasizes the role of the family in proclaiming the Gospel?

- What would it be like to equip parents with the knowledge and skills to share their faith with other parents?
- What would it be like to engage the family in projects and experiences that put faith into action through engagement in church ministries and service to the wider community?

 See chapter 3 for family catechesis strategies.

Life Stage or Peer Group Catechesis

The *Directory for Catechesis* recognizes that each life stage presents unique life tasks and situations, needs and interests, and spiritual-religious needs and faith journeys that catechesis must address. The *Directory* offers a person-centered approach that recognizes that each stage of life presents opportunities and challenges for faith growth. It proposes "pathways of catechesis" that vary based on the life situation of the person.

...The Gospel is not intended for humanity in the abstract, but for each human being, real, concrete, historical, rooted in a particular situation and marked by psychological, social, cultural, and religious dynamics, because "each one is included in the mystery for the Redemption." For one thing, faith is not a linear process and it participates in the development of the person, and this in turn influences the journey of faith. It cannot be forgotten that every phase of life is exposed to specific challenges and must confront the ever-new dynamics of the Christian vocation. (224)

It is therefore reasonable to offer pathways of catechesis that vary based on the participants' different needs, ages, and stages of life. So it is indispensable to respect anthropological-developmental and theological-pastoral realities, taking into account the educational sciences. This is why it is pedagogically important, in the process of catechesis, to attribute to each stage its own importance and specificity.... (223)

Catechesis is fashioned around the life stages (and/or peer groups) with content, methods, formats, and approaches that address the diverse life tasks and situations, needs and interests, and spiritual and faith journeys of people across the life cycle. At each stage of life, catechesis is responsive to the unique features and characteristics, milestones and transitions; the unique features of ethnic cultures; and the diverse spiritual and religious lives of people today.

Catechesis addresses the needs of each stage of life through:

1. a *variety of content*, programs, activities, and resources;

2. a *variety of learning methods* to address the whole person and how he or she learns best;

3. a *variety of catechetical formats* for learning (on your own, with a mentor, at home, in small groups, in large groups, in the church community, and in the community and world)

delivered in physical gathered settings, online settings, and hybrid settings; and

4. a *variety of schedules* by offering programming in synchronous and asynchronous modes and making programming available anytime and anywhere.

APPLICATION: LIFE STAGE / PEER GROUPS

How can your parish structure catechesis at every stage of life to incorporate the three faith-forming environments—intergenerational, family, and peer group—so that people can experience their reinforcing influence every year through relationships, experiences, programs, and activities?

- What would it be like if the annual plan for children and adolescent catechesis incorporated all three environments?

    » *Intergenerational* faith-forming experiences such as Sunday Mass, seasonal celebrations, intergenerational learning, mentoring relationships with older members, ministry opportunities in the Church, and more

    » *Family* faith-forming experiences: whole-family programs at church, grandparent-grandchild activities, activities for faith practices at home, family-centered sacramental preparation, and more

    » *Peer group* (or age group) faith-forming experiences such as classes, courses, retreats, Vacation Bible School, mission trips and service activities, and more

- How can your parish structure catechesis so that families with children, young people, and adults could select from a menu of faith-forming experiences that include intergenerational, family, and peer group

activities and create their own annual plan for participation?

- How can your parish incorporate a variety of content, programs, and resources; a variety of learning methods; a variety of catechetical formats; and a variety of scheduling for catechesis at every stage of life?

*See Practice Resource #4: Programming Approaches for Catechesis at **ncclcatholic.org/ guided-by-the-directory**.*

See chapters 4, 5, and 6 for children, adolescent, and adult catechesis strategies, respectively.

4 Catechesis speaks to the needs, traditions, and spirituality of each culture in the parish and designs approaches to address the uniqueness of each culture.

Catechesis engages each distinct culture in the parish by getting to know deeply the culture of persons, understanding how the Gospel and the faith is already present in each culture, recognizing the significance of popular piety as it celebrates the faith, and, together with people of each culture, developing catechesis that speaks to the needs and spirituality of each culture. In the words of the *Directory*:

With respect to the inculturation of faith, catechesis takes into consideration the following guidelines:

- getting to know deeply the culture of persons, activating relational dynamics marked by reciprocity that fosters a new understanding of the Gospel;

- recognizing that the Gospel possesses its own cultural dimension through which over the course of the centuries it has inserted itself into the different cultures;

- communicating true conversion that the Gospel, as a force for transformation and regeneration, effects within cultures;

- making it understood that seeds of the Gospel are already present in cultures, although it is not exhausted in them;

- making sure that the new expression of the Gospel according to the culture being evangelized does not neglect the integrity of the contents of the faith, an important factor in ecclesial communion. (397)

The heart of catechesis with cultural communities is inculturation of the Christian message, a process that brings the transforming power of the Gospel to touch persons in their hearts and cultures at their deepest levels. It involves listening to the culture of the people for the echo of the word of God.

Catechesis communicates the Christian message through patterns of thought, history, culture, and experience so that various cultures perceive the good news as addressed to them in their own uniqueness and concrete situations. This includes inspiring identity and pride in the riches of the cultures in order to bring them forth as an offering of gifts to the larger community, as well as developing and using culturally appropriate catechetical methods, tools, texts, and resources.

Catechesis is responsive to the uniqueness of communities by incorporating cultural festivals and holidays, traditions, values, customs, history, language, and practices, *and* integrating the unique culture with the Catholic faith and teachings.

Catechesis incorporates culturally relevant stories, lives of the saints and holy people, and creative expression—art, music, dance, and other forms to communicate the Gospel and Catholic tradition. Storytelling and narrative approaches are a powerful tool for transmitting the Good News and Catholic faith in cultural communities.

Catechesis recognizes that cultural communities may have distinct learning styles and preferences, and it utilizes educational methods best suited to the learning styles and preferences of cultural groups.

APPLICATION

How can your parish design catechesis that engages each distinct culture in your community by doing the following?

- Getting to know deeply the culture of persons

- Understanding how the Gospel and the faith is already present in each culture

- Recognizing the significance of popular piety, cultural traditions and stories, festivals and holidays, art and music in transmitting and celebrating the Catholic faith

- Using learning methods best suited to cultural groups

5 Catechesis builds a culture of full inclusion in the life of the Church and all catechetical programming for persons with disabilities, utilizing educational methods that meet the needs of children and young people with disabilities.

The *Directory for Catechesis* emphasizes the full inclusion of person with disabilities in catechetical programs, reception of the sacraments, and the life of the parish community.

Communities are called not only to take care of the most fragile, but to recognize the presence of Jesus who in a special way manifests himself in them. This "calls for twofold attention: awareness of the possibility to educate in the faith the people with even grave or very grave disabilities; and a willingness to consider them as active subjects in the community in which they live." (269)

It is the task of the local Churches to be open to the reception and ordinary presence of persons with disabilities within programs of catechesis, working for a *culture of inclusion* against the logic of the disposable. Persons with intellectual disabilities live out their relationship with God in the immediacy of their intuition, and it is necessary and ennobling to accompany them in the life of faith. This requires that catechists seek new channels of communication and methods more suitable for fostering the encounter with Jesus. It is therefore useful to employ experiential dynamics and languages that involve the five senses and narrative methods capable of involving all the participants in a personal and meaningful way.... (271)

Persons with disabilities are called to the fullness of sacramental life, even in the presence of severe disorders. The sacraments are gifts from God, and the liturgy, even before being rationally understood, needs to be lived; therefore no one can refuse the sacraments to persons with disabilities.... Pastoral inclusion and involved in liturgical action, especially on Sundays, is therefore important. Persons with disabilities can become adept in the lofty dimension of the faith that includes sacramental life, prayer, and the proclamation of the Word. In fact, they are not only recipients of catechesis, but participants in evangelization. It is desirable that they themselves should be catechists and, with their testimony, transmit the faith in a more effective way. (272)

The National Catholic Partnership on Disability (NCPD) (**https://ncpd.org**) recommends that every parish can help persons with disabilities feel valued, welcome, and affirmed within the context of each of these five areas:

1. Accessibility and attitudinal: being aware of and naming our discomforts, fears, and assumptions

2. Language of inclusion

3. Accessibility and hospitality: physical and social

4. Meaningful participation in the parish community: nurturing lifelong spirituality, living a full sacramental life, identifying and aligning individual gifts for ministry to the parish community and the local community

5. Belonging: moving from inclusion to belonging and relationships

NCPD believes that the best teaching practices include flexible grouping, adaptive materials, and natural supports. Formats include the following:

- Typical Program or Session: young person participates in a typical setting with peers without extra help or adaptations.

- Program Supports: young person participates in a typical setting with adapted material and an aide.

- Learning Support Program: young person participates in small-group learning with adapted curriculum.

- Individualized Program: young person is catechized independently and joins peers for prayer, liturgies, and special activities.

NCPD recommends educational methods that respond well to the learning needs of children and young people with disabilities:

- blended learning that uses technology and hands-on materials

- shorter segments of instruction

- smaller groups of learners

- the incorporation of music and movement

- multisensory approach (the engagement of all five senses)

- use of visuals and three-dimensional objects

- maintaining a routine

- reliance on simpler and fewer words

- small, handheld objects (fidgets)

APPLICATION

How can your parish become more inclusive and accessible to people with disabilities?

How can your parish utilize effective teaching practices (flexible grouping, adaptive materials, and natural supports) to structure catechesis for persons with disabilities?

How can your parish implement educational methods that are designed for the learning needs of children and young people with disabilities?

6 Catechesis views human experience as integral to catechesis—in its identity and process, in its content and methods— as it seeks to help illuminate and interpret people's experiences of life in the light of the Gospel.

The *Directory for Catechesis* presents the role of human experience this way: "Human experience is integral to catechesis, in its identity and process, but also in contents and method, because it is not only the place in which the word of God is proclaimed but also the space in which God speaks" (197).

Catechesis recognizes that in order to make the Christian message intelligible to people of all ages, "catechesis must value human experience, which persists as a primary form of mediation for getting to the truth of Revelation" (200).

Catechesis utilizes methodologies that are inspired by the pedagogy of Jesus. "In his proclamation of the Kingdom, Jesus *seeks*, *encounters*, and *welcomes* people in their concrete life situations. In his teaching as well he begins from the observation of events in life and history, which he reinterprets for a sapiential perspective. There is something spontaneous about how Jesus assumes lived experience which shines through in the parables especially" (198).

Catechetical methodologies seek to draw upon people's own lived experiences as a space in which God speaks; share the word of God through Scripture and Tradition; and encourage them to integrate their lives and faith into a living Christian faith. In this way, catechesis is both kerygmatic and experiential. Catechesis is most effective as it presents every aspect of the faith tradition to refer clearly to the fundamental experiences of people's lives. Catechesis constantly integrates life and faith toward lived faith.

The methodology of *life experience to faith tradition to life application* promotes an integrated approach to education, where faith is woven into all aspects of learning and living.

1. *Life experience*: Acknowledging and understanding the real-world contexts in which people live; and recognizing that catechesis should be relevant to people's lives and experiences.

2. *Faith tradition*: Integrating the Bible and Catholic tradition and teachings in the catechetical process; and helping people develop a deeper understanding of their faith and how it can inform their thoughts, actions, and decisions.

3. *Life application*: Encouraging people to apply their faith and learning to their real-life situations; seeing how faith can be

lived in various aspects of life, including relationships, family, work, community, and the world.

APPLICATION

How can your parish utilize catechetical methodologies with each age group that views human experience as integral to catechesis—in its content and methods—because it is the "place where the word of God is proclaimed and space in which God speaks"?

How can catechesis with each age group use a learning process that moves from life experience to the faith tradition to life application?

7 Catechesis utilizes a variety of processes and methods for educating and forming people in the faith and for the faith in ways that are appropriate to the age and intellectual development of people.

The *Directory for Catechesis* encourages parishes to use methods informed by the latest research and practice on learning today; and employ the most effective learning strategies and methods for educating and forming people in the faith and for the faith in ways that are appropriate to the age and intellectual development of people.

> Catechesis does not have a single method but is open to evaluating different methods, engaging in pedagogy and didactics and allowing itself to be guided by the Gospel necessary for recognizing the truth of human nature. "The age and the intellectual development of Christians, their degree of ecclesial and spiritual maturity and many other circumstances demand that catechesis should adopt widely differing methods." (195)

Since the Church does not have a method of her own for proclaiming the Gospel, an effort of discernment is needed so as to test everything and keep what is good (cf. 1 Thes 5:21). Catechesis can evaluate, as it has done throughout history, methodological approaches centered more on the realities of life or based more on the message of faith. This depends on the concrete situations of the subjects of catechesis. (196)

There has been extensive research on how people learn best. Learning sciences research has identified many of the most effective practices for learning—some targeted to specific age groups, but many that apply to learning with all ages. These practices, methods, and tools can be utilized to design catechetical programming and learning experiences that respond to the ways people learn best today.

All of the research points to a central principle: *learners are at the center of the learning experience*. Everything is designed around the learner. All learning components are designed for the educational experience to be adaptable to the needs and potential of each learner and to support the highest possible outcomes for each learner. Learning programs and environments recognize the learners as the core participants, encourage their active engagement, and develop in them an understanding of their own activity as learners. Learning activities allow learners to construct their learning through engagement and active exploration.

A second key principle is *learner variability*. No two people learn in the same way. Each person has different experiences to draw from to master content, create meaning, work in groups, share, and achieve potential. Learner variability is the recognition that all learners differ, and learning sciences research shows that these differences matter for learning.

Catechetical programming uses the latest research on effective learning to incorporate methods that are most effective in promoting learning. The following ten methods reflect the latest research on learning.

1. *Personalized learning* tailors the learning environment—what, when, how, and where people learn—to address the individual needs, skills, and interests of each person.

2. *Differentiated instruction* takes into account that learners in a single group may be at different starting points in their learning process and may require a combination of different content and methods to encourage learning.

3. *Active learning and engagement* involves learners with the material through discussions, problem-solving, hands-on activities, simulations, teaching others, or other active methods.

4. *Practice-oriented learning* recognizes that people learn by doing—that they learn more deeply when they apply knowledge to real-world problems and when they take part in projects that require sustained engagement and collaboration.

5. *Collaborative learning* enhances understanding through interaction, experiences, discussion, and shared learning activities with their peers.

6. *Project-based learning* helps learners gain knowledge and skills by engaging in real-world application through meaningful projects in group settings.

7. *Multiple intelligences learning* provides learning experiences with a variety of ways to learn: verbal-linguistic, logical-mathematical, visual-spatial, bodily-kinesthetic, musical-rhythmic, naturalist, interpersonal, and intrapersonal.

8. *Multisensory, multimodal learning* engages all the senses—sight, taste, smell, touch, and hearing—in learning experiences.

9. *Microlearning* provides short-form learning experiences (five to fifteen minutes) where content is developed in small learning units to enhance comprehension and retention of knowledge, skills, and practices

10. *Dual coding learning* combines visual and verbal information, such as using diagrams or images alongside written or spoken explanations.

APPLICATION

Select a target age group or catechetical program and examine how often your parish uses these ten methods in catechetical programs. Then, reflect on the results of your review. Which methods are you using? Which methods do you need to begin using? How could you transform a program to incorporate one or more of these methods?

*Use Practice Resource #5: Assessment: Using Contemporary Methods for Catechesis to explore how you can use the ten methods at **ncclcatholic.org/guided-by-the-directory**.*

8 Catechesis in a digital culture utilizes a variety of new digital tools and approaches, including online learning and hybrid models of learning that integrate online and face-to-face learning in physical settings.

The *Directory for Catechesis* recognizes the challenges the new digital culture presents for the Church and the Catholic faith (see 359–372), but it also recognizes the opportunities presented by the new technologies.

Within the Church, there is often a habit of one-directional communication: preaching, teaching, and the presentation of dogmatic summaries. Moreover, the written word alone struggles to speak to the young, who are used to a language consisting of a combination of written word, sound and images. Digital forms of communication instead offer possibilities, in that they are open to interaction. This is why, along with technological knowledge, it is necessary to learn effective approaches to communication and to guarantee a *presence on the internet* that bears witness to the evangelical vision. (214)

It is good for communities…to respond to the new generation with the tools that are already in common use in teaching. It is also a priority for catechesis to educate believers in the good use of these tools and a deeper understanding of digital culture, helping them discern the positive aspects from the ambiguous ones…. (216)

The digital transformation has created more options for programming. Catechetical programming can now be designed in three modes (or spaces): 1) *gathered physical settings* (churches, homes, camps, retreat centers, community places, colleges, or seminaries); 2) *online settings* (websites, social media, online communities, online classrooms, and more); and 3) *hybrid settings* that combine physical gathering with online content and experiences. (See Practice Resource #6: Using Digital Methods in Catechesis for more examples of digital approaches.)

One Program in Three Modes

With multiple ways to program in physical, online, and hybrid spaces, one program or experience can be designed in all three spaces, increasing the availability to a wider audience of people while not increasing the number of unique programs a parish creates. The choice is no longer whether to participate but which option best suits a person's time, schedule, and learning preferences. Here is an example of a program that is conducted in multiple formats: same program, with multiple ways to experience it.

1. *Large-group physical gathering*: People gather at church and a leader facilitates the program—making a presentation (or having a guest presenter) or showing a video, providing time for people to read and reflect, and guiding small groups in discussing the content.

2. *Small-group physical gathering*: People gather in small groups in homes or coffee shops or another conducive setting, watch the video, read and reflect on the content, and discuss the content.

3. *Small-group hybrid*: People watch the video on their own, then gather online in a small group (Zoom or other video conferencing platform) to reflect and discuss the content.

4. *Online with interaction*: People complete the sessions on their own and share reflections in a Facebook group (asynchronous) or meet on Zoom to discuss the program (synchronous).

5. *Online independent*: People complete the learning program on their own.

Hybrid Models of Catechesis

Hybrid models of catechesis hold together two important values in faith formation: 1) the importance of in-person relationships and faith-forming experiences and 2) the importance of being responsive to the complexity of people's lives and their religious-spiritual needs. Hybrid models expand faith formation opportunities for everyone. Parishes can become much more intentional about when, where, how, and why they gather because they can now integrate online with in-person faith forming. The key to hybrid catechesis is the integration of in-person faith forming with online faith forming in one holistic integrated experience.

One way to develop a hybrid model is to begin with gathered program in a physical setting and then deepen it with resources and activities online. Consider extending Sunday Mass with online activities on the Sunday lectionary readings and the season of the Church year. Consider providing online formation that extends and deepens the experience of an in-person class, program, or event.

A second way to develop a hybrid model is to begin with online catechesis, leading to in-person experiences. This approach is known as *flipped learning*, in which direct instruction moves from the group learning space to the individual learning space online, and the group space is transformed into a dynamic interactive learning environment where the leader/teacher guides participants as they creatively discuss, practice, and apply the content. One example of this approach is an adolescent Confirmation program that developed a monthly format that included:

- *On your own*: Engaging in learning with a monthly playlist—watching videos, reading short articles, praying, writing reflections in a journal—on the theme.

- *In a small group*: Participating in one small-group experience (online) to discuss the content in the playlist and what they are learning.

- *In a large group*: Gathering for a monthly program at church with all groups for community sharing, interactive activities, short presentations, and ideas for living faith in daily life.

Online-Only Learning

Parishes can develop fully online catechetical programming (asynchronous) by offering independent (on-your-own) faith formation using the abundance of online programs and resources for all ages, especially adults. Leaders can curate courses and resources to organize playlists or web pages with self-directed learning topics like Scripture, prayer and spiritual formation, social justice issues, theological themes, morality and ethics, and much more.

Churches can develop a complete online faith formation experience with content and experiences, such as an online Advent or Lent curriculum that connects the seasonal events at church with online content for experiencing the season in daily and home life. The online experiences can include prayer activities, daily Bible readings, daily devotions, study resources, videos, and service activities.

Churches can use video conferencing to create webinars, such as a monthly theology presentation for adults or a monthly one-hour parent formation. A parent webinar series can be designed around the knowledge, skills, and practices for faith forming and effective parenting and can use guest presenters to conduct the webinars. A church could blend the monthly webinars with one or two parent dinners (with child care or parallel children's programming provided) during the year for parents to gather in person to meet each other and discuss what they are learning through webinars.

APPLICATION

How can your parish more effectively utilize digital methods and tools in catechetical programming with families and all ages?

How can your parish utilize the "one program in three modes" approach to catechetical programming? Which programs can serve as a pilot for this approach?

Where are the opportunities for offering hybrid catechetical programming in your parish? Which programs can be transformed from a gathered-only model into a hybrid model? Which new programs can be designed in a hybrid model?

Where are the opportunities for providing online-only catechesis for a distinct audience or age group?

Use Practice Resource #6: Using Digital Methods in Catechesis for more examples of how you can use digital methods.

CHAPTER 2
PRACTICE RESOURCES

You will find the following Practice Resources at **ncclcatholic.org/ guided-by-the-directory**:

PRACTICE RESOURCE #2
Assessment: Applying the Directory for Catechesis to Parish Life

PRACTICE RESOURCE #3
A Guide for Applying the Eight Practices from the Directory to Parish Catechesis

PRACTICE RESOURCE #4
Programming Approaches for Catechesis

PRACTICE RESOURCE #5
Assessment: Using Contemporary Methods for Catechesis

PRACTICE RESOURCE #6
Using Digital Methods in Catechesis

Catechesis with Families

PART 1. **Exploring the Vision of Catechesis with Families in the Directory for Catechesis** (PARAGRAPHS 224–235)

Chapter VIII in the *Directory*, "Catechesis in the Lives of Persons," begins with catechesis and the family, presenting the family as central to catechetical ministry and the Church's future. "The family is a community of love and of life, made up of a complex of interpersonal relationships…through which each human person is introduced into the human family and into the family of God which is the Church" (226).

A family is the first community and the most basic way in which God gathers us, forms us, and acts in the world. The family is the primary mechanism by which a Catholic identity becomes rooted in the lives of young people through the day-to-day religious practices and the ways parents model their faith and share with their children.

The *Directory* presents family catechesis in three ways: catechesis *in* the family—focusing on parents nurturing faith; catechesis *with* the family—focusing on the parish community forming the faith of families; and catechesis *of* the family—focusing on the family proclaiming the Gospel. These ways can form the foundation and framework for family catechesis in parish communities.

*Catechesis **in** the family* emphasizes the central role of the family in nurturing faith.

> The family is a proclamation of faith in that it is the natural place in which faith can be lived in a simple and spontaneous manner. It has a unique privilege: transmitting the Gospel by rooting it in the context of profound human values. On this human base, Christian initiation is more profound: the awakening of the sense of God; the first steps in prayer; education of the moral conscience; formation in the Christian sense of human love, understood as a reflection of the love of God…It is a Christian education more witnessed to than taught, more occasional than systematic, more ongoing and daily than structured into periods. (227)

*Catechesis **with** the family* emphasizes the role of the parish community in forming the faith of families, centered on the kerygma.

> The Church proclaims the Gospel to the family....At the present time, catechesis with families is permeated by the kerygma because in and among families the Gospel message should always resound....This message has to occupy the center of all evangelizing activities. Moreover, in the dynamic of missionary conversion catechesis with families is characterized by a style of humble understanding and by a proclamation that is concrete, not theoretical and detached from personal problems. The community, in its efforts to bring evangelization and catechesis into families, marks out paths of faith that should help them to have a clear awareness of their own identity and mission: it therefore accompanies and supports them in their task of transmitting life, helps them in the exercise of their inherent duty of education, and promotes an authentic family spirituality. In this way the family is made aware of its role and becomes, in the community and along with it, an active participant in the work of evangelization. (230)

*Catechesis **of** the family* emphasizes the role of the family in proclaiming the Gospel.

> As a domestic church...the Christian family takes part in the Church's mission and is therefore an agent of catechesis. The work of handing on the faith to children, in the sense of facilitating its expression and growth, helps the whole family in its evangelizing mission. It naturally begins to spread the faith to all around them, even outside the family circle. In addition to its natural service of child-rearing, the family is therefore called to contribute to the building up of the Christian community and to bear witness to the Gospel in society. (231)

The *Directory for Catechesis* recognizes that there are important times in the life of the family when people more readily allow themselves to be touched by God's grace and become open to making a journey of faith (232). Among the examples when the parish community needs to be especially attentive are preparation for marriage, catechesis of young married couples, catechesis of parents at their child's baptism, catechesis of parents with children, and intergenerational catechesis (see paragraph 232).

Reflecting on Catechetical Practice

1. The three areas of family catechesis can form the foundation and framework for family catechesis in your parish community. How *does* catechetical ministry in your parish community currently put into practice the three areas of family catechesis in the *Directory*?

- Catechesis *in* the family—focusing on parents nurturing faith
- Catechesis *with* the family—focusing on the parish community forming the faith of families
- Catechesis *of* the family—focusing on the family proclaiming the Gospel

2. How *could* catechetical ministry in your parish community put into practice the three areas of family catechesis in the *Directory*? Imagine the possibilities.

3. How *does* catechetical ministry in your parish address the important times in the lives of families as described by the *Directory*?

- Preparation for marriage
- Catechesis of young married couples
- Catechesis of parents at their child's baptism

- Catechesis of parents with children
- Intergenerational catechesis

4. How *could* catechetical ministry in your parish address the important times in life of families as described by the *Directory*?

*To learn more about the research on families and faith formation, go to Practice Resource #7: Practices for Forming Faith with Families at **ncclcatholic.org/ guided-by-the-directory**.*

PART 2. **Designing Catechesis with Families Inspired by the *Directory for Catechesis***

How would you envision and design catechesis with families around the specific life-stage needs of families with young children, grade school children, young adolescents, and older adolescents that is informed by the vision and practices of the *Directory for Catechesis*?

The following ideas flow from the vision and practices in the *Directory*. They are offered to stimulate your imagination and begin the process of envisioning new approaches for catechesis with families.

Develop a Two-Decade Plan for Family Faith Formation

Catechesis with families can implement an intentional, continuous plan for forming the faith of families from birth to high school graduation in four life stages—young children, grade school children, young adolescents, and older adolescents—with age-appropriate faith-forming programs, activities, and resources.

This two-decade plan focuses on faith forming at home, family-involving faith-forming experiences at church, and parent (and grandparent) formation in parenting for faith.

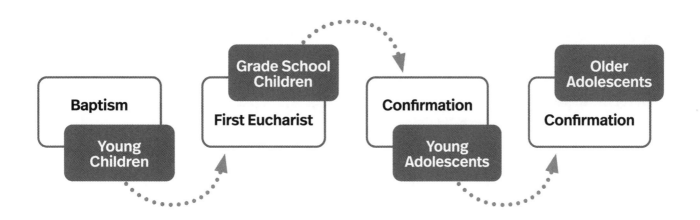

Seven Elements of Faith Formation

A family plan is a holistic approach to forming faith in the first two decades of life by integrating several essential elements in developmentally appropriate ways at each life stage. These seven elements can form a template for designing programs, activities, and resources.

1. Developing faith practices at home by reading the Bible, learning the Catholic tradition, praying, celebrating rituals and milestones, celebrating the seasons of the Church year, serving those in need, working for justice, caring for creation, eating together, having family faith conversations, providing moral instruction, and more

2. Worshipping God with the parish community at Sunday Mass

3. Celebrating sacraments, rituals, and milestones at home and at church

4. Celebrating Church year seasons at home and at church

5. Developing parenting practices and skills appropriate to each stage of life

6. Developing the knowledge and skills for parenting for faith growth

7. Participating as a family in family catechesis programming and parish gatherings

A two-decade plan includes a life-stage progression of parent workshops, webinars, classes, activities, support groups, and resources from infancy through the end of the adolescent years that provides parent faith formation, equips parents to be faith formers of their young people, and develops the knowledge and skills for effective parenting.

With new digital tools and media, parishes can reach today's parents and families anywhere and anytime with engaging and interactive content. Each new stage of a parent plan could be introduced through a variety of educational opportunities and

then sustained through support groups, continuing education, and online resources and activities.

Life Stage Plan

- Birth: parenting young children

- Start of school: parenting grade school children

- Middle school: parenting young adolescents

- High school: parenting older adolescents

- Graduation from high school: parenting emerging adults

Incorporate sacramental preparation for Baptism, First Eucharist, and Confirmation into a two-decade plan for family faith formation, using the catechumenal model of preparation, celebration, and mystagogy.

See Practice 2 in chapter 2 for additional background on the catechumenal model of formation.

The catechumenal model of formation provides a holistic formation process that includes:

- A first proclamation of the Gospel (kerygma)

- A comprehensive introduction to the Christian life

- Liturgies, rituals, and symbols that engage the heart and the senses

- A community of faith and support

- Apprenticeship and mentoring in faith

- Engagement in the mission of the Church and service to the world

- Formation that fosters conversion of heart and mind in a new way of life

- Ever-deeper formation in faith and the life of the community (mystagogy)

Using the catechumenal process, catechesis can be *personalized* around people's religious faith and practices:

1. Those who have a vibrant faith and relationship with God and are engaged in a faith community

2. Those who participate occasionally in the faith community and whose faith is less central to their daily lives

3. Those who are uninvolved in a faith community and who value and live their spirituality outside of organized religion

4. Those who are unaffiliated, have left involvement in organized religion, and have little need for God or religion in their lives.

The catechumenal process can offer catechesis for those who need "taste and see" experiences, "refresher" experiences, "growing" experiences, and "going deeper" experiences. (See Practice 1 in chapter 2 for additional information.)

Catechumenal Process for Baptism

Three Pathways through "Remote" Preparation

1. For parents who have not been active in their faith life and practice: provide a first proclamation of the Gospel (kerygma) and then an introduction to the Christian life.

2. For parents who need a refresher: provide an introduction to the Christian life.

3. For parents who are growing in their faith: provide an exploration of the areas of the Christian life where they need growth.

"IMMEDIATE" PREPARATION FOR ALL PARENTS

- Catechesis on Baptism: theology, rituals, and symbols

- Engagement with a community of faith and support—other parents or families and the intergenerational faith community

- Mentoring by members of the faith community

CELEBRATION OF BAPTISM

CONTINUED GROWTH AND ACCOMPANIMENT (MYSTAGOGY)

- A continuous plan for family forming from Baptism to First Eucharist using the seven elements of faith forming (see above)

- Continuing parent formation

- Continued mentoring and support for parents

- Continued engagement with a community of faith and support

Catechumenal Process for First Eucharist

Three Pathways through "Remote" Preparation

1. For parents and children who have not been active in their faith life and practice: provide a first proclamation of the Gospel (kerygma) and then an introduction to the Christian life.

2. For parents and families who are active and growing in their faith: provide an exploration of the areas of the Christian life where they need growth.

"Immediate" Preparation for All Parents

- Catechesis on the sacrament of Eucharist: theology, rituals, and symbols

- Family-centered preparation for the whole family—large group or parent/family small groups

- Family retreat experience

- Engagement with the intergenerational faith community and Sunday Mass

CELEBRATION OF THE SACRAMENT

CONTINUED GROWTH AND ACCOMPANIMENT (MYSTAGOGY)

- Family catechesis programming in the parish

- A continuous plan for faith formation at home using the seven elements of faith forming

- Parent formation

- Continued mentoring and support for parents

- Continued engagement with a community of faith and support

For an illustration of a catechumenal approach to the Sacrament of Confirmation, go to Chapter 5: Catechesis with Adolescents.

Family Strategies

1 **Engage the whole family in family catechesis programming.**

Family catechesis can be designed as the *primary* model for catechesis with families (monthly, twice a month, or weekly); as an *integrated* model within age-group programming and/or within the seasons of the year (Advent, Lent, and more) and/or as family workshops throughout the year; and as family-centered *sacramental preparation* (Reconciliation and First Eucharist).

The family catechesis learning process typically involves five elements in an extended time format for for ninety minutes to two hours.

1. A shared meal

2. A shared prayer experience

3. A whole-family learning experience on the topic of the program with content and methods appropriate to all ages

4. An in-depth learning on the topic which can be conducted in three different ways:

    a) the whole family learning together with activities appropriate to all ages

    b) parallel groups (children, teens, parents) learning at the same time with content and learning activities appropriate to each age group

    c) learning activity centers with whole family and age-specific learning activities

5. A closing whole-family activity to discover how to apply their learning to daily life using resources and activities provided in print or digital formats

Family Catechesis as the Primary Model

Family catechesis as the primary learning model for parents, children, and young teens is developed around monthly or yearly themes drawn from the Creed, sacraments, morality, justice and service, prayer and spiritual life, Church year seasons, Scripture, Christian practices, and more.

Family catechesis models blend gathered experiences (at church or in family small groups in homes or other settings), at-home faith formation, and online resources. They can be structured and scheduled in several ways to respond to the needs of a parish community, such as monthly, twice monthly, or weekly programming. Here are a few examples:

Monthly Plan with a family session and at-home faith formation:

WEEK #1. Family session at church or in small groups of families (1.5 to 2 hours)

WEEK #2. At-home faith formation with online resources

WEEK #3. At-home faith formation with online resources

WEEK #4. At-home faith formation with online resources

Monthly Plan with a family session, at-home practice, and age-group learning:

WEEK #1. Family session at church or in small groups of families (1.5 to 2 hours)

WEEK #2. At-home faith formation with online resources

WEEK #3. Age-group learning session at church for children, young teens, and parents (1.5 hours)

WEEK #4. At-home faith formation with online resources

Twice-Monthly Plan with a family session and at-home faith formation:

WEEK #1. Family session at church or in small groups of families (1.5 to 2 hours)

WEEK #2. At-home faith formation with online resources

WEEK #3. Family session at church or in small groups of families (1.5 to 2 hours)

WEEK #4. At-home faith formation with online resources

Weekly Plan with family sessions at church or in small groups of families:

In the Weekly Plan, the movements of the learning process are assigned to individual weeks. Over a month, the entire learning process is experienced. Each session is usually one hour in length.

WEEK #1. A whole-family learning experience with content and methods appropriate to all ages

WEEK #2. An in-depth learning conducted in one of three ways: a) the whole family learning together with activities appropriate to all ages in the family; b) parallel groups (children, teens, parents) learning at the same time, with content and learning activities appropriate to each age group; c) learning activity centers with whole family and age-specific learning activities

WEEK #3. A whole-family activity to discover how to apply their learning to daily life using resources and activities provided in print or digital formats

WEEK #4. At-home practice with online resources

Family Catechesis in an Integrated Model

An *Integrated Plan* incorporates family catechesis within the age-group curriculum for grades 1 to 8. The themes for family catechesis can flow from the age-group curriculum or focus on core faith themes and Church year seasons. Here is an example of a four-week sequence:

WEEKS #1–3. Age-group catechesis

WEEK #4. Family learning experience (This continues throughout the year.)

A *Seasonal Plan* is built around the Church year seasons and feasts—Advent, Christmas, Lent, Holy Week, Easter, Pentecost, All Saints/All Souls, and more. Family catechesis sessions are incorporated into the schedule of the year so that age-group programs and activities are not scheduled during a family catechesis program. A Season Plan is an excellent way to introduce family catechesis to the families and the parish community.

A *Workshop Plan* is designed around family life skills that will strengthen family life and around parent–child/teen relationships, such as communicating effectively, discussing tough topics, making decisions and solving problems as a family, learning how to build strong relationships and express care for each other, supporting each other (encouraging and praising, giving feedback, standing up for each other), and treating each with respect and dignity. A Workshop Plan can provide occasional family or parent-only gatherings throughout the year. Workshops can also be designed as mini-conferences (e.g., three hours) on a Saturday or Sunday, with a general session for the whole family and breakout sessions for parents, children, and teens.

2 Cultivate the development of faith practices at home through developmentally appropriate formation programs, activities, and resources.

Cultivating faith practices at home includes reading the Bible, learning the Catholic tradition, praying, celebrating rituals and milestones, celebrating the seasons of the Church year, serving those in need, working for justice, caring for creation, eating together, having family faith conversations, and providing moral instruction.

There are many ways that parishes can cultivate the development of faith practices at home. Here are a few examples to stimulate your own thinking.

- Incorporate formation in faith practices into existing programming, such as sacramental and milestones celebrations; age-group programming; Sunday worship and after-worship programming; service projects, mission trips, retreats, and camps.

- Make a faith practice the focus of each month or the season of the year through family or intergenerational learning, worship and preaching, and service/action. For example, during the Lenten season, the church community and family can focus on one or more practices that reflect the theology and liturgies of the season, such as forgiveness,

discernment, prayer, and service. Combine the at-church experience with activities for families to do at home.

- Develop a year-long focus on a practice such as the "Bible story of the month" to introduce important stories and teachings in the Bible by teaching the practices for reading, interpreting, praying, and applying the scriptures to their lives. Select twelve of the most relevant and developmentally appropriate Bible stories for each age. Integrate the Bible teaching into one session or program each month. Provide online resources for parents to reinforce the Bible story online: reading the story, watching the video, discussing the story.

- Develop a family faith formation website with playlists for the "practice of the month" with engaging activities—print, audio, video, apps—tailored to families with young children, older children, young adolescents, older adolescents, and the whole family, as well as "how to" information and videos for parents. The website can serve as a resource center with content and activities and as a portal to curated ideas on other websites.

- Create immersive experiences on faith practices for families. Design extended-time programs (half-day, full-day) where families can experience a practice firsthand, such as hospitality at a homeless shelter, serving a meal at a soup kitchen, or caring for creation by planting a garden. Combine the at-church experience with activities for families to do at home.

3 Equip and resource families to grow in faith through participation in Sunday Mass and the seasons of the Church year by connecting the Sunday experience to daily life at home.

Catechesis for families designed around the Lectionary readings or the Church year season can be structured around a variety of resources that help families experience, reflect on, and apply the theme from Sunday to their family life throughout the week. For example:

- Family conversation questions on the theme of the Sunday readings

- Activities for the Church year feast or season

- Weekly table ritual

- Podcast or video of the sermon with a study guide for the parents, children's creative Bible activities, storybooks, video presenting the Bible story

- Daily prayer, weekly family devotion
- Short Bible reading for each day of the week, online resources for studying the Bible (print, audio, video)

4 Engage families in serving those in need, caring for creation, and working for justice.

There are local, national, and global organizations that provide ready-to-use educational resources and action projects that a parish can adopt to create their programs. Programs can be designed just for families or for the whole parish community, providing a great way to integrate families into the community and create intergenerational relationships and community. Here are three examples:

- *An Annual Family or Church-Wide Service Day*. Create a four-week program that culminates on a Sunday where families or the entire parish community engage in service projects in and with the community. Develop an annual theme, such as poverty, care for creation, or peacemaking. Select a local and global project already developed by a justice or service organization. Prepare families or the whole community for the service engagement, utilizing the resources developed by the partner organizations. Include 1) worship and prayer experiences focused on the particular theme or project; 2) educational sessions, including social analysis of the issues and reflection on the teachings of Scripture and the Christian tradition; 3) household activities on the theme or project, such as prayers, learning resources, and action suggestions; 4) a website with the resources, activities, action projects, and features to allow people to share what they are doing; and 5) special presentations by experts on the issues and by people engaged in action on the issue.

- *A Monthly Family or Intergenerational Service Project*. Using the same design as the church-wide service day, develop a monthly service project that addresses one need or issue (local and/or global) each month. Each month's project can include a short educational program of the topic, an action project, and reflection on the project. Themes for the service projects can correspond with calendar events and seasons, as well as Church year seasons. Examples include Back to School (September) and school kits for students; Thanksgiving (November) and feeding the hungry; Martin Luther King Jr. Day (January) and serving or respecting human dignity; Lent (February or March) and serving the poor; Earth Day (April) and caring for creation.

- *Family or Intergenerational) Service Nights at Church*. Service nights are simple, self-contained programs that feature five to ten service-activity stations that engage families and all ages in doing a simple project for the benefit of a group in need. At one learning center, people might create greeting cards for the elderly or sick church members. At another, they might make blankets for a homeless shelter, or bake cookies or make sandwiches for a soup kitchen, or package kits for homeless people. Many organizations provide the logistics for designing the learning centers.

Parent Strategies

Here are several things to keep in mind when designing and leading effective programs and experiences for parents.

- Create a supportive, caring environment for learning. Greet parents, provide time for them to get acquainted with one another, and encourage mutual support during and after the experience.

- Engage parents actively in the learning. The amount they learn will be in direct proportion to how much they put into the experience.

- Let parents be the experts. Show that you value their knowledge and experience by giving them opportunities to contribute to the learning experience.

- Connect the learning activities to the parents' experiences and values so they know "this is for me and about my family."

- Focus the content on real needs, issues, and concerns, not just on content that parents ought to know. For example, if you want to help parents teach their child/teen about healthy concepts of right and wrong, first identify the ways this connects with parents' needs or concerns regarding moral values, then develop the experience to reflect those concerns.

- Include information and skills parents can put into action immediately. Such application reinforces what they learn and helps parents internalize it.

- Have parents practice the new skills. Demonstrate how to use skills and practice during the program so that parents have a direct experience of how to use the skills or practice at home.

1 Focus on parents as the most significant influence on the religious and spiritual outcomes of young people.

The content of parents' programming, resources, and support needs to incorporate what we know from research about the ways that parents influence the spiritual and religious life of young people. Here are five important findings to incorporate in programming:

- Nurture and encourage parents' personal faith and practice.

- Develop skills and practices for building close and warm parent–child relationships.

- Encourage and support parent involvement in church life and Sunday Mass.

- Strengthen parents' role in modeling and teaching a religious faith.

- Equip parents (and grandparents) with faith-forming skills and practices.

2 Address the diverse motivations of parents for support, education, and formation by providing meaningful and relevant opportunities that speak to their motivations.

- *Transmission of values*: Many parents are motivated by the desire to pass on their religious values, beliefs, and traditions to their children. They see religious learning as a way to ensure that their children share their faith.

- *Sense of identity*: Parents often view religious learning as a means of helping their children develop a strong sense of identity, belonging, and cultural heritage.

- *Moral and ethical development*: Religious teachings often emphasize moral and ethical values. Parents are motivated by the belief that these teachings can help instill positive values and guide their children's behavior.

- *Connection to community*: Parents are motivated to involve their children in religious learning to connect them with a supportive and like-minded community of faith.

- *Future well-being*: Some parents are motivated by the belief that religious learning will contribute to their children's overall well-being and happiness in life.

- *Respect for cultural heritage*: Parents who value their cultural heritage may be motivated to provide their children with a connection to their cultural traditions through religious learning.

- *Character development*: Parents often see religious teachings as a way to help shape their children's character, fostering qualities like empathy, compassion, and humility.

- *Guidance for challenges*: Some parents are motivated by the belief that religious teachings can provide guidance and comfort for their children as they face life's challenges.

- *Community and social engagement*: Parents may see religious learning as a way for their children to become active participants in their religious community and engage in community activities.

- *Parent–child bond*: Engaging in religious learning together can create meaningful opportunities for parents to bond with their children and share experiences.

3 Equip parents with the knowledge and skills for passing on religious faith and practice so they can incorporate faith practices into the day-to-day religious practices of the family.

Raising religious children is primarily a practice-centered process, not chiefly a didactic teaching program. Certain faith practices make a significant difference in nurturing the faith of children and adolescents at home, especially:

- Reading the Bible as a family and encouraging young people to read the Bible regularly

- Praying together as a family and encouraging young people to pray personally

- Serving people in need as a family and supporting service activities by young people

- Eating together as a family

- Having family conversations about faith

- Talking about faith, religious issues, and questions and doubts

- Ritualizing important family moments and milestone experiences

- Celebrating holidays and Church year seasons at home

- Celebrating milestones and sacraments in the lives of individuals and the whole family

- Providing moral instruction

- Being involved in the parish community and participating regularly in Sunday Mass as a family

4 Equip parents with the knowledge and skills for developing quality relationships with their young people and applying styles of parenting that make a difference in faith transmission.

- Cultivating relationships of warmth and love, which make everything else possible

- Balancing religious firmness with religious flexibility in their parenting so as to maintain more positive relationships with their children

- Transmitting their faith to their children while honoring their agency by teaching principles and values, providing expectations of religious participation and responsibility, not forcing faith, allowing exploration and mistakes, and showing respect for children's views

- Talking about religious matters during the week: when parents talk about their religion in personal terms, that sends a strong message to their kids that it's important to them

- Practicing an "authoritative" parenting style (as opposed to authoritarian, permissive, or uninvolved style) by maintaining and enforcing high standards and expectations for their children while simultaneously expressing a lot of open warmth and connection to their children, and confidently giving them enough space to work out their own views and values

- Listening more and preaching less. It is a more satisfying and successful religious and relational experience when the conversations are more child/youth-centered than parent-centered

5 Equip parents with the most important knowledge and skills for effective parenting.

- Expressing care to young people by listening to them, being dependable, encouraging them, and making them feel known and valued

- Challenging young people by expecting them to do their best and live up to their potential

- Providing support for young people by encouraging their efforts and achievements and guiding them to learn and grow

- Treating young people with respect, hearing their voices, and including them in decisions that affect them

- Inspiring young people to see possibilities for their future, exposing them to new experiences and places, and connecting them to people who can help them grow

- Demonstrating a warm and affirming parenting approach

- Creating a warm, caring, supportive family environment

- Practicing effective communication skills

- Managing screen time and social media use

- Learning effective discipline practices

6 Provide parent mentors (or coaches) who can offer guidance and support for parents and the whole family at each stage of life from birth through the end of adolescence.

Mentors can accompany parents and families in their spiritual lives, guiding them in growing in their relationship with God and learning more about the faith. Mentoring can be life-cycle specific, with mentors who focus on children or adolescents. Parent mentors can be drawn from the grandparent generation who are actively engaged in church and bring decades of parenting and family life experiences. Churches can provide training for mentors (mentoring skills, understanding today's family, learning how to access online resources and activities).

7 Offer affinity groups for parents in online and physical settings.

Provide opportunities for parents with children in the same age group to talk about parenting, get information and encouragement, and discuss family life issues and challenges. Churches can offer groups for mothers, fathers, single parents, divorced parents, parents in blended families, parents of children with disabilities, and more.

CHAPTER 3
PRACTICE RESOURCES

You will find the following Practice Resources at **ncclcatholic.org/ guided-by-the-directory**:

PRACTICE RESOURCE #7
Practices for Forming Faith with Families

PRACTICE RESOURCE #8
Parish Family Faith Formation Assessment

PRACTICE RESOURCE #9
What's Your Parish's Approach to Families?

PRACTICE RESOURCE #10
Models of Family Catechesis

Catechesis with Children

PART 1. **Exploring the Vision of Catechesis with Children in the *Directory for Catechesis*** (PARAGRAPHS 236–245)

Early childhood is a critical time in which openness to God and having a life of faith is either encouraged and fostered or discouraged. The life of the family at this stage is also important as they get used to a new family member and shift into new roles as parents of a growing family. In the preschool years, the parts of the brain that are most responsible for feelings of relationships and attachment are growing rapidly. Chapter XIII of the *Directory* reminds us that:

> It is from the tenderest age that the child must be helped to perceive and to develop the sense of God and the natural intuition of his(her) existence. Anthropology and pedagogy confirm, in fact, that the child is capable of relating to God and that his(her) questions about the meaning of life arise even where the parents are hardly attentive to religious education. Children have the capacity to pose meaningful questions relative to creation, to God's identity, to the reason for

good and evil, and are capable of rejoicing before the mystery of life and love. (236)

Catechesis for young children at this stage introduces them to Jesus as both God and friend and to the parish community as an extended family. As parents realign many aspects of their lives as they begin a family, parishes have a unique opportunity to reach them and walk beside them. The *Directory* states:

> *Early childhood*, or pre-school age, is a definitive time for the discovery of religious reality, during which children learn from their parents and from the environment of life an attitude of openness and acceptance or of aversion and exclusion toward God.... When from an early age the child is in contact, in the family or other surroundings in which he(she) grows, with different aspects of the Christian life, the child learns and internalizes an initial form of *religious socialization* in preparation for the forms that come later

for the development of Christian moral conscience. At this age [catechesis] is a matter of first evangelization and proclamation of the faith in an eminently educational form, attentive to developing a sense of trust, of gratuitousness, of self-giving, of invocation and participation, as a human condition onto which is grafted the salvific power of faith. (239)

Catechesis in middle childhood focuses on initiation into all aspects of Christian life and is reinforced by the witness of the Christian community in the parish.

Middle childhood (ages 6-10), according to a long-standing tradition in many countries, is the period in which Christian initiation begun with baptism is completed in the parish. The overall itinerary of Christian initiation is meant to convey the main events of salvation history that will be the object of more in-depth reflection as the child gets older, and to gradually make him(her) aware of his(her) identity as the one who has been baptized. Catechesis...is also attentive to the existential conditions of children and to their questions of meaning. The journey of initiation provides, in fact, for a teaching of the truths of faith that is reinforced with the witness of the community participation in the liturgy, the encounter with the word of Jesus in Sacred Scripture, the beginning of the exercise of charity. (240)

Ages six and seven are often the beginning of formal catechesis for children. At this age, they are beginning to move beyond a focus on self, so it is an appropriate time to introduce them to Jesus and how to have a relationship with him. It is also an appropriate time to encourage positive relationships with the church community. Children at this age are focused on rules, so this is also a good time to introduce basic teachings of our faith and even God's rules and guidelines for living as a follower of Jesus. Children preparing for First Eucharist can better understand that the Eucharist is not just bread and wine but Jesus' body and blood. As the child grows older, peers become very important to them, making this a good time to teach them about the parish community and the larger Catholic Church. And as a child reaches ages nine and ten, they are gaining a sense of right and wrong and learn from doing. Modeling faith for them is important, as is having them look at certain situations and practice making good choices.

The *Directory* stresses that faith takes time, happens in stages, and happens within community.

The need to make the process of Christian initiation an authentic experiential introduction to the entirety of the life of faith leads to looking at the catechumenate as an indispensable source of inspiration. It is entirely appropriate to *configure Christian initiation according to the formative model of the catechumenate* but with criteria, contents, and methodologies adapted for children. The gradation of the process of Christian initiation for the young inspired by the catechumenate provides for times, rites of passage, and active participation at the Eucharistic table that constitutes the culmination of the initiatory process. (242)

Most importantly, the *Directory* reminds us that the parish community should dialogue with parents when possible as we support them in their faith formation of children. We need to hear from them and be present to them to provide support and encouragement. In doing so, we will be proclaiming and manifesting God's goodness and love for them (238).

Catechesis with children can be challenging, and it can be difficult to reshape our thinking and our models to effectively share the Gospel with them and their families.

- How does catechetical ministry in your parish community guide children in growing in the Catholic faith and practicing their faith in daily life?

- How effective are your current catechetical approaches in nurturing the faith of children? In nurturing the faith of the whole family?

- How effective is your catechetical ministry in engaging children (and their parents) in parish life and developing an experience of belonging?

PART 2. **Applying the Practices of Catechesis with Children Inspired by the *Directory for Catechesis***

How would you envision and design catechesis with young children (0–5), grade school children (6–10), and their parents, informed by the vision and practices of the *Directory for Catechesis*?

The following ideas flow from the vision and practices in the *Directory* and are a response to the challenges of the new context. They are offered to stimulate your imagination and begin the process of envisioning new responses for catechesis with children.

1 Develop catechesis with children guided by the research on the most important contributors to faith forming with children.

Discovering and nurturing a child's spirituality is crucial at this stage in their development. It helps them embrace faith and faith practices later in life. We owe it to every child to help them discover and respond to God's loving and gracious presence in their life. This faith formation process culminates when a young person or young adult makes a personal decision to make their faith and religious practice *central* to their identity and life.

What does the body of literature show are the most important contributors to effective faith formation with

children? The experts in the field of children's spirituality and faith formation identify four broad and intertwining contributing factors.

- *Meaning-making.* Effective faith formation with children recognizes that they are continually processing their experiences, making meaning of them, even if they cannot express or articulate the meaning. They have an innate spiritual sense and are predisposed to spiritual, God-connected meaning-making. Even if adults don't understand, children regularly construct concepts based on their experiences, and when these are applied to the spiritual landscape, they begin to grasp big-picture concepts such as *God is good, God loves me, God is real and present in my life.*

  Children approach meaning-making through a combination of verbal communication, play, story, art, and mirroring behaviors in which relationships are a critical link between engagement and articulation of understanding. We can get a glimpse of how children perceive God simply by asking them to draw a picture of God.

- *Discovery.* Through creative play, story, and imagination, catechesis provides ample opportunity for children to develop and form their own relationships with God and with others who believe in God. Effective faith formation with young children is not linear or strictly tied to curriculum. But that does not mean it is without planning or forethought. Encounter is primary. A child's encounter with Jesus leads to a natural desire to learn more about God.

- *Conversation.* Conversation is an important element in the process of spiritual discovery. Children need to be allowed space to dialogue, listen, and question. In doing so, they will engage in meaning-making as they share with one another.

- *Posture of family and Church.* Spirituality is an innate capacity. It cannot be taught. It must be supported and cultivated through lived experiences and meaningful relationships. Historically, such support has been offered by families as well as religious communities and schools. Children have strengths and gifts to offer the whole community. While they

possess spiritual capacity, they still require significant and nuanced guidance.

What does the body of literature show are the activities, tasks, and behaviors that contribute to and bolster faith formation with children? Catechetical leaders need to create a culture of joy, welcome, wonder, discovery, exploration, imagination, and meaningful learning. To create this culture and foster the desire to learn about God, we need to keep in mind these tasks.

- *Having a multidimensional view.* We need to keep children's strengths and vulnerabilities in mind and prepare adults to facilitate their spiritual growth *and* to learn from them. This mindset equips adults to welcome children in the church community and family with a healthy mutuality and encourages church communities to plan for and benefit from offering both age-specific and multigenerational faith experiences.

- *Creating intentional experiences.* Through a variety of activities, children can explore, engage, and express their faith in unique ways. These should engage emotions as well as cognitive faculties where children can engage both physically and intellectually. Consider faith-related games and Bible story skits or plays.

- *Using open-ended stories and parables.* Jesus taught using parables, frequently without explanation. When leaders allow children to discover God through open-ended presentations of parables and narratives, they foster children's natural strength of opening meaning in contrast to adults' proclivity to close meaning.

- *Playing.* We engage children in creative play, relationship building, independent and cooperative play, spontaneous prayer, and much more.

- *Processing experiences.* Children need tools to process their experiences and discoveries. Tanya Campen suggests using these six tools:

  1. *Story.* Story invites children into a time and space where they can do the holy work of active wondering and meaning making.

  2. *Liturgy and Ritual.* The words, actions, and rhythm that make up our time together and are the tools for a child's meaning making process.

  3. *Relational Awareness.* Through their actions, wondering, and work, it became clear that children are very aware of themselves, others, and God.

  4. *Memory Markers.* Children's ways of remembering what they have experienced and learned as they do the holy work making meaning.

  5. *Wonder.* Creating a place for children to wonder and use their imagination is essential to their meaning-making process.

  6. *Work.* The child begins to identify their work and begins seeking ways to respond with faithful action.

     (Tanya Campen. *Holy Work with Children: Making Meaning Together.* Eugene, OR: Pickwick Publications, 2021. See chapter 6.)

- *Participating in Mass.* When we find ways for children to both participate and lead us in worshipping at Mass, we discover that they are capable. When children are given the opportunity to enter a holy space and meaningfully participate in liturgy, they respond. Children can read Scripture, sing, pray, welcome people, and give announcements. This participation fosters belonging and helps faith to become real in their lives.

APPLICATION

Do we have an adequate understanding of children's spiritual development?

Do we recognize children as multi-faceted human beings and create space and a culture for authentic wonder and discovery?

Do we set them on a lifetime journey of faith and religious practice?

Do we advocate for children and their families, and do we offer empathy and understanding for the complexities at this stage in life?

*To learn more about the research on children and faith formation, go to Practice Resource #11: Practices for Forming Faith with Children at **ncclcatholic.org/ guided-by-the-directory**.*

2 Incorporate the ways that Generation Alpha (2012–) children learn into all catechetical programming and experiences.

As the Alpha generation is relatively young, their learning preferences are still emerging and evolving. Based on research in the learning sciences and current trends and observations, there are characteristics that can guide effective learning approaches for this generation.

- *Personalization and adaptability*: Alpha children benefit from personalized learning pathways tailored to their individual needs and interests.
- *Incorporate technology thoughtfully and with limits*: Leverage technology to connect with them but be mindful of its potential pitfalls. Use interactive apps and educational games to provide information, foster discussions,

and create virtual communities. Create digital assessments using games based on their lessons, or group games like *Jeopardy*.

- *Short attention spans*: The abundance of information and stimuli in the digital age has contributed to shorter attention spans among Alpha children. Learning experiences that are broken into smaller pieces, concise, visually appealing, and interactive can help maintain their focus.
- *Multimodal learning*: Alpha learners respond well to diverse forms of media and content. Utilize a mix of text, images, videos, and audio to cater to their different learning preferences.
- *Hands-on and experiential learning*: Alpha learners benefit from hands-on and experiential learning opportunities. Incorporate practical activities, experiments, simulation games, and real-world experiences to deepen their understanding, such as a hunger banquet for the families or a project in which the children build a model of a just society with materials you give them.
- *Visual and spatial learning*: Visual content, such as infographics, diagrams, and animations, can be particularly effective in conveying information to Alpha children, as they are drawn to visually stimulating and colorful materials.
- *Collaborative learning*: The Alpha generation is growing up in a highly connected world. Encourage collaborative learning experiences, both in person and through digital platforms, to promote teamwork and communication skills. Create skits, role-playing experiences, problem-solving activities, team games, and more.
- *Interactive*: Interactive experiences can foster better understanding and engagement.

Encourage discussions, questions, and activities that allow them to apply their faith to real-life situations. Engage in "What if?" questions and allow for open discussion.

- *Encourage curiosity and exploration*: Alpha children are naturally curious and eager to explore. Create a learning environment that fosters curiosity, creativity, and problem-solving skills. Don't be afraid to move outside as well. Do a prayer walk, a creation exploration, or a "Where do I see God?" exercise.

- *Encourage critical thinking*: Foster their ability to think critically about their faith, beliefs, and the world around them. Encourage them to ask questions and explore different perspectives. Affirm and encourage different opinions.

- *Emphasize emotional intelligence*: Foster emotional intelligence and social skills through activities that promote empathy, understanding, compassion, friendship, and emotional expression.

- *Play-based learning*: For the youngest Alpha learners, play-based learning can be an effective approach to engage their imagination and cognitive development.

- *Storytelling*: Stories are a powerful tool for teaching moral and spiritual lessons. Share age-appropriate stories from the Bible that resonate with their experiences. Have them act out Bible stories or draw them as they understand the stories.

- *Address difficult questions*: Alpha Generation children are exposed to diverse perspectives and challenging questions early on. Address their doubts and questions in an open, respectful, and age-appropriate manner.

3 Utilize the process of the catechumenal model in sacramental preparation for Baptism and First Eucharist using a three-movement process of preparation, celebration, and mystagogy.

See chapter 3, part 2, for a description of a catechumenal approach to Baptism and First Eucharist.

4 Implement a comprehensive plan for forming the faith of families with young children (after Baptism) with age-appropriate programs, activities, and resources to guide the family from birth through the start of school (age 0–5).

Every six months, from birth to five years old, parents can receive age-appropriate faith-forming resources (print, audio, video, digital) to use with their children and parenting tips for the new phase of their child's growth, published on the family faith formation website and communicated via email or text.

- *Developing faith practices at home*: reading the Bible, learning the Catholic tradition, praying, celebrating the seasons of the Church year, serving those in need, working for justice, caring for creation, eating together, having family faith conversations, providing moral instruction, and more

- *Celebrating milestones*: birthdays, Baptism anniversaries, "first" milestones, entry to preschool and kindergarten, and more

- *Parenting knowledge*: understanding young child development and practices for effective parenting of young children

- *Parenting for faith skill*: reading a Bible story, praying with a young child, having faith conversations, answering difficult questions, and more

- *Online groups for parents of young children:* forums, chat rooms, online groups, social media
- *Mentors from the church community* (e.g., grandparents) to accompany parents on the journey from Baptism to start of school
- *Gatherings for parents and for families* at *church*

5 Provide a holistic curriculum for grade-school children that provides a rich menu of faith-forming experiences each year, incorporating intergenerational, family, and children's programs and activities.

 See the five tasks of catechesis in chapter 1.

 See Practice #7 in chapter 2 for more information on programming.

Catechesis with children, guided by the *Directory,* incorporates *five tasks of catechesis:* knowledge of the faith, celebration of the mystery (liturgies and seasons of the liturgical year), forming for life in Christ (moral life), prayer, and active engagement in community life.

A menu approach has 1) a variety of content, programs, activities, and resources; 2) a variety of formats—on your own, mentored, small groups, and large groups; 3) a variety of times to participate and scheduling options (synchronous and asynchronous); and 4) hybrid, online, and gathered modes of programming.

A menu approach provides a way to structure learning with experiences, programs, and activities designed to promote growth in faith for people who want to grow deeper in the faith, for those who are inquiring or aren't sure the Christian faith is for them, and for those who don't need God or religion in their lives.

Families with children could select from a menu of faith formation experiences to create their plan for the year or for a season of the year. The menu would include:

- *Intergenerational* faith-forming experiences: Sunday Mass, seasonal celebrations, intergenerational learning, mentoring relationship with older members, ministry opportunities in the church, family service projects, and more
- *Family* faith-forming experiences: whole-family programs at church, grandparent–grandchild activities, activities for faith practices at home, and more
- *Age group* faith-forming experiences: classes, courses, retreats, Vacation Bible School, Christmas play, service activities, and more.

Churches can establish participation guidelines for families and children so that each year or season, they would select a certain number of intergenerational experiences, family at-home activities, and children's programs at church.

The menu approach puts families and children at the center of faith formation and gives them choices over what and when and where they will learn. The variety of offerings is more appealing, as is the flexibility of the program options. It moves away from one-size-fits-all catechesis for children. A menu approach provides the opportunity for variety, choice, flexibility, intentional community, and personalization.

6 Engage grade-school children and their parents (and grandparents) in a family catechesis program.

Use family catechesis as a primary model for children's catechesis (monthly or twice a month), addressing all of the foundational themes and topics

of children's catechesis. Family catechesis models usually incorporate the following elements:

1. A shared meal

2. Shared prayer experience (ritual action, prayer, video)

3. A whole-family learning experience on the topic of the program, with content and methods appropriate to an all-ages audience

4. In-depth learning on the topic can be conducted in three different ways: a) the whole family learning together, with activities appropriate to all ages, that gives parents a chance to learn how to share their faith with their children; b) parallel groups learning at the same time, with content and learning activities for age groups and a parent group; and c) learning activity centers, with whole-family and age-specific learning activities at a variety of stations or centers.

5. A closing whole-family activity and sharing to discover how to apply their learning to daily life using resources and activities provided in print or digital formats

6. Resources to take home for continued learning and practice

 See chapter 3, Family Strategy #1, for examples of family catechesis models.

7 Provide environments that allow children to encounter the living God directly.

Children's relationship with God is shaped and formed by the way they experience God through goodness, beauty, wonder, and awe; through relationships with other people, nature, art, wonder, and mystery; through the woundedness of human experience that opens them to God's healing presence; through Jesus' life and how he modeled the way God intends us to live.

Parishes can provide safe and trusting environments for children to experience prayer in a variety of forms and settings, to participate actively in Sunday Mass, to experience the liturgical seasons, to celebrate rituals and sacraments, to participate in retreat experiences, to serve people in need, to care for creation, and more. Children can experience God through hands-on participation in the life, ministries, and activities of the parish community according to their abilities.

Catechesis guides children's participation by providing them with resources—language, practices, rituals, habits—that enable them to participate with all their senses in the life of the community. This restores the connection between learning and practice—precisely what is missing in the traditional model of classroom learning, where the material presented stands divorced from the practice of faith. It also overcomes the age segregation so prevalent in churches today.

8 Create safe spaces for children to wonder, discover, and make meaning.

Catechesis seeks to create a space in which children can share their stories, practice wondering, use their imaginations, and learn from the entire community. Rather than attempting to *give* children faith, creating spaces for wonder, discovery, and meaning-making nurtures the spiritual presence that is already in the lives of children. Nurturing spiritual growth in children includes recognizing the Divine presence in their lives. It involves nurturing the spiritual growth process and guiding all children as they make meaning from their experiences and relationships. Spiritual growth honors the individual child and affirms their particular developmental process.

Catechesis helps children to know, interpret, and incarnate the faith. It provides an intentional space where teachers and children share their faith stories with each other, engage in intentional theological reflection, and use developmentally appropriate methods that help every child learn, make meaning, and respond to their experience with the Holy. We do this by creating a safe space where children are valued and respected and by inviting them into the process of learning through claiming and responding to God's presence in their lives.

Through intentional and authentic conversations, children and adults find space to listen to God and to discern how they might respond to all they are hearing and experiencing. Through this process, we encourage children and model for them how to do the work of meaning-making, not by giving them information but by inviting them and guiding them, by sharing stories and asking questions, by inviting them to share stories and ask questions, and by listening to what they say.

Programs such as a Play & Worship for ages three to five allow for such learning and inquiry, as do Bible camps and other programs that allow for play, creativity, and learning all in one. A faith-oriented summer project based on the book *Flat Stanley* encourages families to bring "Flat Jesus" with them on their summer vacation and share with the community via social media how they celebrate Jesus being present with them as a family.

As children *engage* in the word and traditions of the Catholic faith, *recognize* the presence of God and others, *claim* their own experiences, and *respond* to these experiences, they make meaning that informs and affects their individual faith narrative. In doing the important work of engaging, recognizing, and claiming God's presence in their lives, children begin to hear God's call to respond, and they know what to do next. In responding to God's grace and love, they enter into another experience, another possibility, continuing their meaning-making in response to this new information and wisdom.

Using these four elements, doing the holy work of meaning-making, and participating in this process, children build their faith narrative and develop religious language to articulate and celebrate how God is working in their lives. Adults support children in this process by modeling language and creating space for them to discover and practice their faith. They encourage children in the work of engaging, recognizing, claiming, and responding to God's presence in their lives.

9 Implement parent formation and education through programs, activities, resources, webinars, and more for parents of children.

 See chapter 3 for parent formation and education strategies.

CHAPTER 4
PRACTICE RESOURCES

You will find the following Practice Resource at **ncclcatholic.org/ guided-by-the-directory**:

PRACTICE RESOURCE #11
Practices for Forming Faith with Children

The *Directory*
highlights the fresh
perspective, energy,
and optimism of
young adolescents
and older adolescents
as well as the role of
the whole community
in the formation of
young people.

Catechesis with Adolescents

PART 1. **Exploring the Vision of Catechesis with Adolescents in the *Directory for Catechesis*** (PARAGRAPHS 244–256)

The *Directory* highlights the fresh perspective, energy, and optimism of young adolescents and older adolescents as well as the role of the whole community in the formation of young people. Guided by Pope Francis' exhortation *Christus Vivit* (Christ is alive!), the Church is called to create and offer catechesis that reflects on the aspects of Jesus' life and mission. Catechesis and faith formation should encourage in all young people a growing relationship with God, an awareness of being part of a family and a church family, and an openness to the Holy Spirit and the mission God gives them.

Using the story of the disciples on the road to Emmaus, the *Directory* stresses accompanying young people in this very formative time in their lives. By nature, young hearts are ready to change and to get up and learn from life. Jesus walks with the two disciples who did not understand the meaning of all that has happened to them. Jesus asks them questions and patiently listens to their version of events.

In doing so, he helps them recognize what they were experiencing all along.

> The togetherness of the Lord Jesus with the two disciples of Emmaus, his walking with them, dialoguing, accompanying, helping to open their eyes, is a source of inspiration for walking with young people. Within these dynamics, the Gospel must be proclaimed to the world of young people with courage and creativity, the sacramental life and spiritual accompaniment must be presented. Thanks to the Church's mediation, young people will be able to discover the personal love of the Father and the companionship of Jesus Christ, and to live out this season of life particularly "suited" to the demands to the great ideals, to generous forms of heroism, to the coherent demands of thought and action. (244)

Pastoral care of adolescents also needs to be characterized by this relational ministry, deep listening, and reciprocity.

Knowledge of the virtual world as well as social media is crucial. Much of humanity is immersed in the digital world on a regular basis. Our digitized and technological culture has profound impact on our ideas, the world, communication with others, and self-understanding. We need to speak the language of young people today. We need to understand how they communicate and learn and search for faith. Digital tools can offer spaces for experiences of faith, but we also need to be aware of the dangers. The *Directory* offers these insights:

> One consideration of a general character regards the question of the language of young people. The new generations are, in general, strongly marked by *social media* and by what is referred to as the virtual world. This offers opportunities that the previous generations did not have, but at the same time it presents dangers. It is of great importance to consider how the experience of relationships mediated by technology may structure the conception of the world, of reality, and of interpersonal relationships. Hence the pressing need for pastoral activity to adapt catechesis for young people, translating the message of Jesus into their language. (245)

Catechesis with Pre-Adolescents (10–14)

Pre-adolescence (or young adolescence) is defined as between the ages of ten and fourteen, a time of movement and passage between the safety of childhood and the perplexities of adolescence. This time in a child's life can be marked with anxiety and confusion as well as great emotional and physical growth. Taking a quick general look at these ages, we see the growing ability to understand signs and symbols and to think more abstractly, the beginning of a question-

ing of their identity and wondering who they will be when they grow older, and growth in their sense of self-consciousness, often with feelings of insecurity.

> Pre-adolescence is the time in which the image of God received in childhood is refashioned: for this reason, it is important that catechesis should accompany this delicate passage and its possible future developments with care seeking help from the research and tools of the human sciences as well. Unafraid of focusing on the essential, the presentation of the faith to pre-adolescents is to take pains to sow within their hearts the seeds of a vision of God that can ripen over time: the illustration of the *kerygma* is to pay special attention to the Lord Jesus as a brother who loves, as a friend who helps one to be one's best in relationships, does not judge, is faithful, values skills and dreams, bringing one's desire for beauty and goodness to fulfillment.
>
> Moreover, catechesis is urged to recognize the self-assertion of pre-adolescents, to create a context in which questions are welcomed and brought into contact with the presentation of the Gospel. The pre-adolescent can enter more easily into the world of Christian experience by discovering that the Gospel touches precisely on the relational and affective dynamics to which he(she) is particularly sensitive. (247)

This can be a time for a deeper exploration of the sacraments and the many rites of the Church. It is also a time for learning how to read and interpret Scripture as a Catholic. Exploring the lives of the saints and their examples of faith is especially helpful as they form their own identity. Young adolescents also begin to question the relevance of faith and what they are learning. Doubts are real, anxieties are prevalent, and the need to belong outweighs most other things. Effective catechesis can create meaningful relationships, comfort, and companionship and can help young people connect faith to their everyday lives.

Catechesis with Adolescents/ Young People (14–21)

Christus Vivit states that youth, as a stage of development, is marked by the growth of personality, dreams which gather momentum, relationships which acquire more consistency, and significant choices (137). This stage in life brings tension between desiring independence and fears of separation from family and becoming an adult. Young people are being called to move forward without cutting themselves off from their roots and to build autonomy within community. They are developing autonomy while continually defining themselves within the views of their peers and cultural constructs. This stage also brings deep questions about identity, true friendships, purpose, and the future. Catechesis is challenged to listen to their questions and share the riches of the Catholic tradition in response. Catechesis guides young people in developing their identity as disciples of Jesus Christ.

It is important to recognize that young people are in *need* of evangelization and are *capable* of evangelizing others through their own witness of faith. Young people can flourish when offered the opportunity to serve and mentor others in roles such as peer ministers. They can make contributions as liturgical ministers and catechists.

Every project of formation which combines liturgical, spiritual, doctrinal, and moral formation is to "have two main goals. One is the development of the *kerygma*, the foundational experience of encounter with God through Christ's death and resurrection. The other is *growth in fraternal love, community life and service*." Catechesis is therefore to present the proclamation of the passion, death, and resurrection of Jesus, the true source

of youthfulness for the world, as a core of meaning around which to build the vocation response. The *vocational dimension* of youth catechesis requires that the pathways of formation be developed in reference to life experience. (253)

Young people have a natural tendency to want to work toward peace, harmony, justice, and mercy in the larger world, and thus for the extension of the kingdom of God. Many young people are willing to commit to initiatives of volunteer work and civic activity and solidarity with others: this social engagement and direct service with the poor are fundamental ways to deepen their faith and discern their life's vocation.

Adolescents are still unsure of who they are as individuals. They may be more self-actualized, but they are still growing, and catechesis needs to address the dynamic of the emergent self. The life of young people is characterized by pressure to perform and achieve, pressure to prepare for adulthood, and the pressures of popular culture. Much of popular culture is often at odds with the Church. Young people are searching for meaning; they feel deep solidarity with others and seek social engagement with the world. Technology and globalization have increased their awareness of the world around them and increased their sensitivities toward people of other cultures and faith traditions. They may express distrust or indifference toward institutions and the Church. They may withdraw from the Church because the way they express their faith is different from what they see in the Church. It is important to create safe spaces for young people to feel comfortable questioning their faith. The process of questioning and struggling is how many young people make the Catholic faith their own.

The pastoral care of youth by the Church is therefore to be first of all a *humanizing and missionary outreach*, which means being capable of seeing the signs of God's love –

and call –in human experience. It is in the light of faith that the search for truth and freedom, the desire to love and be loved, personal aspirations and the impassioned commitment to others and to their world find their authentic meaning. In helping young people to discover, develop, and live their life plan according to God, pastoral care of youth is to adopt new styles and strategies.

It is necessary "to become more flexible: inviting young people to events or occasions that provide an opportunity not only for learning, but also for conversing, celebrating, singing, listening to real stories, and experiencing a shared encounter with the living God." Catechesis with young people as well, therefore, is to be defined by the features of this pastoral style. (252)

A ministry to, with, for, and by youth has a different style, pace, and method. It is flexible and goes to where young people are active. (*Christus Vivit*, 230) It encourages young people to be leaders in their neighborhoods and other settings. Catechesis can happen outside the Church, where it can be relational and grounded in the daily life of young people. The *Directory* encourages us in this mindset:

In addition to organized and structured catechetical programs, catechesis should also be valued when it is carried out in a casual manner in the life environments of young people: school, university, cultural and recreational associations. (254)

Most importantly, catechesis in this fashion is to be open to all, inclusive, and welcoming of all young people who have a desire to encounter God and find community within our walls.

Young people need adults who can guide them through their questions to a faith that is personally meaningful to them. Research shows that young people are most likely to remain committed to their

faith if they have meaningful relationships with adults other than their parents who are intentionally living out their faith.

Faithful adults and parents accompanying young people at this stage are essential. Young people need to be respected in their desire for freedom but also accompanied in their journey. Adolescents crave authentic relationships with adults. Parishes can identify, call, and equip adults who are joyful about their faith to walk beside them as they grow in faith.

In their journey of faith, adolescents need to have convinced and compelling witnesses by their side...the drop in church attendance that often happens during the adolescent years depends not so much on the quality of what was present to them during their childhood–as important as all this is–as having something joyful and meaningful to offer for the younger ages.... Adolescents need priests, adults, and older peers in whom they can see a faith lived out with joy and consistency. (249)

Young people can serve in a variety of roles within the parish community, including as catechists and peer leaders. A parish community can invest in the formation and training of young leaders, helping them recognize their talents and gifts and equipping them to utilize those gifts in the service of others. As the *Directory* states,

Recognition must be given to the value of the creative and co-responsible contribution that young people themselves make to catechesis. The catechetical service of young people is a stimulus for their very growth in the faith. (255)

REFLECTION

Catechesis with pre-adolescents and adolescents can be very challenging, but it can also be richly rewarding and exciting. It can be difficult to move between formal programming and a more open and invitational pastoral style of catechesis, but it is worthy of consideration.

- How does catechetical ministry in your parish community guide adolescents in growing in the Catholic faith and practicing their faith in daily life?
- Does your parish utilize a variety of catechetical approaches and methods?
- How effective are your current catechetical approaches in developing the faith of adolescents? In nurturing the faith of the whole family?
- Do you have trained adult mentors and teachers who accompany youth in the faith journey and serve as models and witnesses of faith?

To learn more about the research on families and faith formation, go to Practice Resource #12: Practices for Forming Faith with Adolescents at **ncclcatholic.org/guided-by-the-directory**.

PART 2. Applying the Practices of Catechesis with Young People Inspired by the *Directory for Catechesis*

How would you envision and design catechesis with pre-adolescents/young adolescents (10–14) and older adolescents/young adults (14–21) informed by the vision and practices of the *Directory for Catechesis*?

The following ideas flow from the vision and practices in the *Directory* and are a response to the challenges of the new context. They are offered to stimulate your imagination and begin the process of envisioning new responses for catechesis with adolescents.

1 Incorporate the ways that Generation Alpha (2012–) and Generation Z (1997–2012) young people learn into all catechetical programming and experiences.

By incorporating these strategies into learning experiences, catechists can create engaging and effective learning opportunities that align with Generation Alpha's and Generation Z's preferences and learning styles, fostering a positive and productive learning environment.

To learn about the characteristics that can guide effective learning approaches for the Alpha generation, go to the first children's catechesis strategy in part 2 of chapter 4.

GENERATION Z LEARNING STRATEGIES

- *Personalized learning*: Tailor learning experiences to individual interests and abilities. Find out what is meaningful to them. Ask them what they want to discuss in youth ministry or on a retreat. This fosters interest and ownership. Create a learning website just for them. Offer relevant prayers, music, appropriate videos that coincide with lessons, and more.

- *Flexibility and autonomy*: Offer flexibility in learning schedules and pathways. Gen Z appreciates the ability to learn at their own pace and on their own terms.

- *Digital and interactive learning*: Gen Z is highly comfortable with technology and often prefers digital learning environments. Utilize online platforms, educational apps, interactive online modules, and virtual simulations to engage them effectively.

- *Microlearning (short and engaging content)*: Gen Z has a shorter attention span due to the rapid information consumption they're accustomed to. Break down content into bite-sized, easily digestible, shorter, and engaging segments using videos, quizzes, and interactive elements. Use apps to play games in gatherings. Have them create video presentations to music or personalized design journals to use in your programs.

- *Visual and multimedia learning*: Incorporate visual aids, infographics, videos, and other multimedia content. Visuals can help convey complex information quickly and effectively. Music is extremely meaningful.

- *Mobile-friendly learning*: Ensure that learning materials are accessible on mobile devices, as Gen Z is accustomed to learning on their smartphones and tablets. You can also use apps to send daily Bible verses or weekly reflections and even create a discussion group. Collaborative and social learning is important and fosters interaction and teamwork.

- *Hands-on experiential learning*: Gen Z tends to learn better through practical and experiential learning opportunities. Provide practical, real-world applications of concepts through projects, simulations, and hands-on experiences. Gen Z learns best when they can apply knowledge in real-world scenarios. Ideas include a hunger banquet or creating Bible skits in today's language. They can recreate a parable or Bible story using text messages in their own language.

- *Feedback and recognition*: Provide regular feedback and recognition for their efforts. Gen Z responds well to immediate feedback and appreciates acknowledgment of their achievements.

- *Purpose-driven learning and context*: Highlight the real-world significance and impact of the learning material. Gen Z is motivated when they understand how their learning can contribute to a better future and how it can be applied to a specific problem or issue. Have them research an issue such as the need for water in developing communities. How would they provide water? Combine local service projects with teaching about the larger worldview of the issue.

- *Creativity and self-expression*: Provide opportunities for Gen Z to express themselves creatively, whether through multimedia projects, storytelling, poetry, drawing, creating videos, finding current music with faith themes, or other forms of self-expression.

- *Critical thinking and problem-solving*: Gen Z values the ability to think critically and solve problems. Include activities that challenge them to analyze information and develop problem-solving skills. Encourage critical thinking by presenting open-ended questions and real-world problems. Social justice issues work well here—share a problem and have them work together to see what they can do or how they can advocate for change. Teach the difference between charity and justice.

- *Sustainability and social responsibility*: Gen Z is particularly concerned about environmental and social issues. Integrate themes of sustainability and social responsibility into the learning content. Again, create projects through which they can learn about local and global issues and create service projects that stress local charity but also encourage them to consider the larger theme of justice.

2 Provide a holistic curriculum for young people that provides a rich menu of faith-forming experiences each year, incorporating intergenerational, family, and youth programs and activities.

 See Practice 7 in chapter 2 for more information on programming.

Catechesis with adolescents, guided by the *Directory*, incorporates *five tasks of catechesis*: knowledge of the faith, celebration of the mystery (liturgies and seasons of the liturgical year), forming for life in Christ (moral life), prayer, and active engagement in community life.

A menu approach has 1) a variety of content, programs, activities, and resources; 2) a variety of formats—on your own, mentored, small groups, and large groups; 3) a variety of times to participate and scheduling options (synchronous and asynchronous); and 4) hybrid, online, and gathered modes of programming.

A menu approach provides a way to structure learning with experiences, programs, and activities designed to promote growth in faith for young people who want to grow deeper in the faith, for those who are inquiring or aren't sure the Christian faith is for them, and for those who don't need God or religion in their lives.

Young people could select from a menu of faith formation experiences to create their plan for the year or for a season of the year. The menu would include: 1) *intergenerational* faith-forming experiences, 2) *family* faith-forming experiences, and 3) *age group* faith-forming experiences.

Churches could establish participation guidelines for young people, so that each year or season they would select a certain number of intergenerational experiences, family at-home activities, and age-specific programs at church. This approach might look like this for a semester time frame:

- Select two in-person catechetical experiences (mini course, one-day program, retreat, etc.) chosen from a list of offerings

- Engage in one service activity or project—alone or with a small group—chosen from a list of projects, followed by an online session to debrief the service experience

- Participate with other generations in a parish-wide activity or take a leadership role in a parish-wide activity

- Participate in two liturgical experiences with other young people or with the whole community: prayer service, special Mass, Stations of the Cross, and more

- Develop a daily prayer practice using one of the resources provided by the parish

The menu approach puts young people at the center of catechesis and gives them choice over what and when and where they will learn. It moves away from one-size-fits-all catechesis for young people. It provides the opportunity for deeper engagement in a topic of their choice, variety, and personalization.

3 Utilize the process of the catechumenal model in sacramental preparation for Confirmation using a three-movement process of preparation, celebration, and mystagogy.

See Practice 2 in chapter 2 for additional background on the catechumenal model of formation.

The catechumenal model of formation provides a holistic formation process that includes:

- A first proclamation of the Gospel (kerygma)

- A comprehensive introduction to the Christian life

- Liturgies, rituals, and symbols that engage the heart and the senses

- A community of faith and support

- Apprenticeship and mentoring in faith

- Engagement in the mission of the Church and service to the world

- Formation that fosters conversion of heart and mind in a new way of life

- Ever-deeper formation in faith and the life of the community (mystagogy)

Using the catechumenal process, catechesis with adolescents can be *personalized* around their religious faith and practices: 1) young people who have a vibrant faith and relationship with God and are engaged in a faith community; 2) young people who participate occasionally in the faith community and whose faith is less central to their daily lives; 3) young people who are uninvolved in a faith community and who value and live their spirituality outside of organized religion; and 4) young people who are unaffiliated, have left involvement in organized religion, and have little need for God or religion in their lives. The catechumenal process can offer catechesis for those who need "taste and see" experiences, "refresher" experiences, "growing" experiences, and "going deeper" experiences.

Sacrament of Confirmation

Three Pathways through "Remote" Preparation

- For young people who are not actively living their faith and have not been involved in faith formation since their First Eucharist: provide a first proclamation of the Gospel (kerygma) and then an introduction to the Christian life. Consider offering a specialized mini-course or retreat experience or a small-group mentored experience focused on an introduction to the Christian faith and the parish community.

- For young people who are actively practicing their faith and have been involved in faith formation: provide a deeper exploration into the Bible and the Catholic tradition in areas of special interest to them.

PREPARATION

- Catechesis on the sacrament of Confirmation: theology, rituals, and symbols—offered in a series of sessions more than once a year, with sponsors invited to journey with the young people and participate in sessions.

- Spiritual formation in the practices of prayer.

- Engagement with a community of faith and support—offered through intergenerational service projects, parish prayer partners, parish-wide liturgies and activities, and more.

- Retreat opportunities offered in different formats and time commitments.

- Mentoring by members of the faith community—creating programming which encourages young people to partner with an adult in short-term formats such as a five-week Lenten faith-sharing series.

CELEBRATION OF THE SACRAMENT

CONTINUED GROWTH AND ACCOMPANIMENT (MYSTAGOGY)

- Preparation for living one's faith in the young adult years

- In-depth catechesis that is interest-based

- Exploration of calling and vocation

- Intergenerational projects in the faith community: e.g., justice, service

- Involvement in leadership and peer ministry

- Continued mentoring

While it may not be feasible to offer three types of "preparation programs," parishes can offer enough variety to address diverse needs and provide pathways for adolescents to grow in faith in ways appropriate to their faith journey. A menu approach to confirmation preparation (see Strategy #2) provides a way to offer specific experiences, programs, and activities designed to promote growth in faith for young people who want to grow deeper in the faith, for young people who are inquiring or aren't sure the Catholic faith is for them, and for those who don't need God or religion in their lives.

Another approach to Confirmation preparation that addresses the busy lives of young people and uses digital approaches to catechesis is the *flipped learning* model. Flipped learning moves direct instruction from the group learning space to the individual learning space online, while transforming the group learning space into a dynamic interactive learning environment where the catechist guides young people as they creatively discuss, practice, and apply the content.

The flipped learning model is very helpful when it is difficult to gather people regularly. Young people can *prepare* online with the appropriate content (experiences, activities, video/audio, and resources); then *engage* in person for the event or program; and *sustain and apply* the experience through online faith formation.

One example of a flipped learning model for the sacrament of Confirmation is illustrated in this monthly format that can be developed into a year-long program:

- *On your own*: Engage young people with a monthly learning playlist—watching videos, reading short articles, praying, writing reflections in a journal—on the theme of the month. There is much content online, or you can create or curate your own.

- *In a small group*: Have young people participate in one small-group experience (online) with an adult facilitator (and a young person who has been confirmed) to discuss the content in the playlist and what they are learning.

- *In a large group*: Involve young people in a monthly meeting with all the small groups for community sharing, interactive activities, short presentations, and ideas for living faith.

 See Practice 8 in chapter 2 for more on digital methods.

See Practice Resource #6: Using Digital Methods in Catechesis at **ncclcatholic.org/guided-by-the-directory**.

4 Immerse young people into the practices that constitute a Christian way of life that address young people's quest for becoming (identity), belonging (relationships and community), and meaning (how to live with meaning and purpose today).

People come to faith and grow in faith and in the life of faith by participating in the practices of the Christian community. They learn the Christian way of life and its practices through experience and through guidance, mentoring, and teaching of other Christians who live these practices.

Consider what it takes to be an actor, musician, artist, dancer, writer, or athlete. They all require developing skills, performing, thinking, and practicing over and over again. While singers and musicians must learn music theory, that is not enough. They have to actually *play* the instrument and *practice*. An artist may know art history and the different forms and styles of painting, but the artist must actually paint and continue to do so to master their craft. Developing a Christian way of life and the practices that constitute that life is a similar process of devel-

oping skills, performing, thinking, and practicing over and over again.

At the heart of Christian practice is Jesus: in his presence and example, a way to live comes into focus. We experience this model of living whenever we celebrate the blessings of life, serve the poor and vulnerable, offer our lives in prayer, forgive others, keep the Sabbath holy, discern God's will for us, or try to transform the world. Christian practices emerge repeatedly in the Bible and Christian tradition, and they have demonstrated their importance in forming a distinctively Christian way of life. Christian practices include caring for creation, discernment, doing justice, dying well, eating well, embracing diversity, finding God in everyday life, forgiveness, healing, honoring the body, hospitality, keeping Sabbath, praying, peace and reconciliation, reading the Bible, serving the poor and vulnerable, stewardship and generosity, and worship.

There are a variety of ways to immerse young people in learning and living Christian practices. These practices can also be added into retreat models and other sessions. Here are two examples.

Christian practice apprenticeships: Identify "practice mentors" in your parish who are living embodiments of a Christian practice, such as service or hospitality or prayer. Develop formation programs around these mentors in individualized and small-group settings where mentors can apprentice young people who want to learn how to live the Christian practice. For example, if people want to learn how to serve people in need at the local homeless shelter, they can accompany the practice mentor when he or she works at the shelter and learn about homelessness and the practice of hospitality and serving others. If a young person wants to learn how to pray, they can be mentored by an adult who has a vibrant prayer life. Each apprenticeship can include a study component to learn about the teachings and examples from the Bible and Christian tradition.

Participants in such a program can gather regularly as a large group to share experiences and learning.

Christian practice learning programs: Through courses, workshops, retreats, action projects, field trips, and practice-focused small groups, provide young people with learning experiences that include:

1. Preparing them with the Scriptural and theological understanding of the practice

2. Engaging them in hands-on experience of the practice (with peers or intergenerationally)

3. Reflecting on the experience and its meaning for them

4. Integrating the practice into their daily lives

Ideas might include the Bible in a year (or season) with a partner, exploring the Gospels or themes of Lent, tending the community garden with their mentor, serving at a soup kitchen, partnering with a nursing home and adopting grandparents, participating in youth masses or Good Friday Stations of the Cross, mission trips that include formation and post-mission reflection with the team, group hikes with Mass outdoors, nature walks, or engaging in service with the homeless directly, such as participating in a program which serves those without homes in your city.

5 Provide safe spaces, small communities, trusted adults, and faith-building skills to guide young people in the process of constructing their identity and faith.

Springtide Research has described a phenomenon of *faith unbundled*—a term that describes the way young people increasingly construct their faith by combining elements such as beliefs, identity, practices, and community from a variety of religious and non-religious sources, rather than receiving all these things from a single, intact system or tradition. Young people with unbundled faith will partake in religion, including practices, beliefs, and communities to the degree that suits them, with no formal or permanent commitment. (*The State of Religion and Young People 2021*, Springtide Research Institute)

Young people are turning to a wide range of traditions, practices, and beliefs when asking and answering important questions about their faith: *What do I believe? Who am I? What is my purpose in the world? What practices have value?* Springtide Research uncovered four characteristics of young people's searching and exploration. They are *curious*, they desire to be *whole*, they deeply crave *connection*, and they value *flexibility*. A question to consider is this: *"How do we allow these things in our models of catechesis for young people?"*

Focus on the big questions in young people's lives and equip them with the skills for constructing a meaningful faith life by drawing upon the Scriptures and Catholic tradition. Consider offering small groups on the big questions, "life-building" workshops with practical skills and tools, retreat experiences for reflection, and more. Having a physical space that young people can call their own is also important. The community has an important place in the accompaniment of young people, and it should feel collectively responsible for loving, motivating, and forming them. It is important that mentors not be judgmental but actively listen and respond with kindness and understanding. Mentors need to be able to acknowledge their own faults and be able to walk alongside young people, nurturing the seeds of faith with genuine care.

6 Provide interest-centered small groups or sessions on a variety of topics that integrate faith and life around the interests and gifts of young people.

Small-group formats provide lots of flexibility in content, schedule, and location (in physical settings, online settings, or hybrid settings). Groups can meet at times and places that best fit young people's lives. They can have short commitments to make it easier for young people to participate. Interest-centered groups can draw upon a wide range of gifts and talents from people of all ages—including young people. Small groups can be developed around a variety of topics, with each one connecting life and faith. Each small group can include a teaching component, along with practice, and performance components. Here are several examples:

- *Life-centered*: preparing for life after high school, dealing with transition, life skills (communication, decision-making), relationships, dealing with loss, and more

- *Creative*: art, music, drama, and more

- *Spiritual*: how to pray, spiritual practices, spiritual direction, and more

- *Biblical*: Bible basics: what's in it, how to read and interpret it, how to understand its history and literary forms, how to seek answers for big questions, and more

- *Action*: serving people in need, responding to justice issues, caring for creation, and doing so together

- *Leadership*: involvement in leadership roles in the church and the community, such as a pastoral council position, retreat leaders, liturgical ministers, and more

- *Theological*: what Jesus means for our life today, how to live morally today, and how to live like Jesus did

7 Implement parent formation and education through programs, activities, resources, webinars, and more for parents of young people.

View parents as partners in the faith development of adolescents. Develop specific ways to Include parents (and the family) in youth programming, Sponsor parent-only sessions that address a variety of parent and adolescent issues, such as mental health issues within the context of faith.

 For more parent formation strategies, see part 2 in chapter 3, on families.

CHAPTER 5
PRACTICE RESOURCES

You will find the following Practice Resource at **ncclcatholic.org/ guided-by-the-directory**:

PRACTICE RESOURCE #12
Practices for Forming Faith with Adolescents

Within the last forty
years, every major
catechetical document,
both from the Vatican
and from the United
States Conference
of Catholic Bishops,
has emphasized
that the education
of adults is at the
center of the Church's
educational ministry.

Catechesis with Adults

PART 1. Exploring the Vision of Adult Catechesis in the *Directory for Catechesis*

Within the last forty years, every major catechetical document, both from the Vatican and from the United States Conference of Catholic Bishops, has emphasized that the education of adults is at the center of the Church's educational ministry. The *Directory for Catechesis* continues that indispensable tradition.

This *Directory* adds to the wealth of research and reflection in highlighting the complexity of adult life today: a "lively dynamism that incorporates the factors of family, culture, and society." Because of this intricacy, today's adult "continually reformulates his(her) own identity, reacting creatively to the different moments of transition that he(she) finds himself(herself) living through" (257).

Of course, the religious dimension is intertwined in the adult journey, taking different forms at various times and in various life happenings. Throughout this journey, faith hopefully becomes "an authentic and continual response to the challenges of life" (257).

What would happen in people's lives, in our parishes, if all our adult faith formation planning and processes began with people's life experiences and then linked these experiences to the blessings, gifts, and challenges of faith?

Adult Approaches to Faith

The *Directory* pays attention to the research and real-life actualities of the varied faith experiences of today's adults, reminding us that each person needs to be "welcomed and listened to in his(her) uniqueness."

The *Directory* cites a few types of adults who live out the faith with different approaches:

- believing adults, who live their faith and want to get to know it better

- adults who, although they may have been baptized, have not been adequately formed or have not brought Christian initiation to completion, and can be referred to as quasi-catechumens

- baptized adults, who although they do not live out their faith on a regular basis, nonetheless seek out contact with the ecclesial community or particular times in life

- adults who come from other Christian confessions or from other religious experiences

- adults who return to the Catholic faith having had experiences in the new religious movements

- unbaptized adults who are candidates for the catechumenate properly so called (258)

REFLECTION

- Do we plan one catechetical program to reach and engage all adults?

- What if we planned catechesis for these distinct groups of adults, realizing that each group has unique needs, questions, and faith experiences?

Tasks for Catechesis with Adults

The *Directory* reminds us that life is a journey and faith is an ever-evolving journey. Adult catechesis is lifelong and all-inclusive. The *Directory* enunciates various tasks for adult faith formation:

- *to elicit faith*, fostering a new beginning of faith-filled experience and making the most of the human and spiritual resources that are never extinguished in the depths of every person, in view of a free and personal resumption of their initial motivation in terms of attraction, gusto, and determination;

- *to purify the faith* from partial, misguided, or erroneous religious representations, helping

the participants above all to recognize the limitations of these and to decide to seek out more authentic distillations of faith in view of the journey toward the fullness of life to which the Gospel calls;

- *to nourish faith* thanks in part to an experience of meaningful ecclesial relationships, promoting the formation of mature Christian consciences capable of giving the reason for their hope and ready for a serene and intelligent dialogue with contemporary culture;

- *to assist the sharing and witness of faith*, preparing spaces of sharing and service to the Church and in the world as ways of realizing the task of manifesting the kingdom of God. (261)

REFLECTION

- What would it look like if catechesis accompanied adults in their continuing journey to adulthood?

- What would it look like if catechesis helped adults to deepen their faith, to live as disciples, and to be active members of the Christian community?

- What would it look like if catechesis empowered adults to be leaven in all areas of society, building the Reign of God?

Criteria for Adult Catechesis

How important is adult catechesis in the priorities of your parish leadership and the adults in the parish community? How does your parish design adult catechesis? Is it about purchasing or adopting a program, or is it designed around the unique needs of adults in the different seasons of adulthood? The *Directory* guides us with some criteria:

- Since the Christian community is a structural element of the catechetical process for the adult and not only its setting, it is necessary that it be capable of renewal, allowing itself to be challenged by the adults of today and their particular concerns as well as being a place of welcome, presence, and support.

- Catechesis of adults needs to propose concrete and characteristic experiences of the life of faith (exploration of Sacred Scripture and doctrine; moments of spirituality, liturgical celebrations, and practices of popular piety; experiences of ecclesial fraternity; missionary exercise of charity and of witness to the world…) that may correspond to the different needs of the human person in his(her) wholeness of affections, thoughts, and relationships.

- Adults must not be considered as recipients of catechesis, but as participants together with the catechists themselves. It is therefore necessary to carry out a respectful welcome of the adults as a person who has already developed experiences and convictions on the level of faith as well, and who is capable of exercising this freedom, developing new convictions in dialogue.

- Catechesis with adults should be attentive to recognizing their situation as men and women, considering the uniqueness with which each one lives out the experience of faith…. (262)

REFLECTION

- How are these criteria alive in your planning?

- What other criteria guide your planning and programming for the adults in your parish?

Forms of Adult Catechesis

So much of adult catechesis is "one-size-fits-all" programming. The *Directory* strongly reminds us that "one size fits all" no longer works. Catechesis must engage a diversity adults' life and faith. For example:

- catechesis as a genuine initiation into the faith, or the accompaniment of candidates for Baptism and the sacraments of initiation through the catechumenal experience;

- catechesis as new initiation into the faith, or the accompaniment of those who, although they have been baptized, have not completed initiation or are not in fact evangelized;

- catechesis as rediscovery of the faith through "listening centers" or other approaches, or a presentation in the vein of evangelization intended for those referred to as fallen away;

- catechesis of the proclamation of the faith in environments of life, of work, of recreation, or on the occasion of demonstrations of popular piety or pilgrimage to shrines;

- catechesis with couples on the occasion of marriage or in the celebrations of sacraments for their children, which often becomes a point of departure for further catechetical experiences;

- catechesis for the exploration of the faith on the basis of Sacred Scripture, a document of the Magisterium, or the lives of the saints and witness to the faith;

- liturgical catechesis, which is aimed at deliberate participation in community celebrations;

- catechesis on moral, cultural, or sociopolitical issues aimed at participation in the life of society, so that this may be active and inspired by the faith;

- catechesis in the area of specific formation of pastoral workers, which constitutes a privileged opportunity for journeys of faith. (264)

REFLECTION

- Many parishes throughout our country are attentive to these various forms of adult catechesis. Which one(s) is most life-giving in your parish?

- Is there one area that has been neglected or ignored?

- What might happen if (one at a time) you renewed and refreshed each area?

- Are there untapped people who might be leaders and/or participants for these areas?

Catechesis with the Elderly

Is adult faith formation a one-and-done endeavor? Are there times we act as though there is a "graduation time"—a time when adults no longer need or desire ongoing formation? There is nothing further from the truth—which the *Directory* emphatically points out: "The elderly must be given adequate catechesis, attentive to the unique aspects of their condition of faith" (268).

As with all adults, older persons are at various places in their faith journey, depending on the circumstances of their life journey; thus, catechesis need to flow from their needs, which will necessitate various and varied opportunities in the parish (and neighborhood).

Our experiences tell us—and Scripture affirms—that our older generations, rich in wisdom, have much to give. Their many life experiences can make them the keepers of memories and tradition. They can "transmit to the young the meaning of life, the value of tradition and certain religious and cultural practices; they bring dignity to the memory and sacrifices of the past generations; they look with hope beyond the difficulties of the present" (268).

REFLECTION

- What if catechesis for older adults helped them to appreciate their innate value and dignity?

- What if catechesis for older adults provided ways for the parish to thank them for their presence?

- What if catechesis for older adults aided them in addressing the questions and challenges of growing older?

- What if catechesis for older adults walked with them in their deepening spirituality?

- What if catechesis for older adults empowered them to continue to serve, perhaps in new ways, by giving back and paying it forward?

GUIDED BY THE DIRECTORY FOR CATECHESIS

PART 2. **Applying the Practices of Adult Catechesis Inspired by the *Directory for Catechesis***

Everything we do teaches. *Our Hearts Were Burning Within Us* (USCCB, 1999) boldly reminds us: "While this pastoral plan is concerned primarily with intentional adult faith formation programs, the success of such efforts rests very much on the quality and total fabric of parish life. This includes, for example, the quality of the liturgies, the extent of shared decision making, the priorities in the parish budget, the degree of commitment to social justice, the quality of the other catechetical programs" (118).

Adult catechesis is not just about planning six-week programs; it is about the way a parish lives moment by moment. The role of the adult faith formation director/committee is the keeper of the flame, to continually ask about all that is happening within the parish (every guideline, practice, activity): How is this affecting the growth, the faith of the adults in our community? "...while the parish may have an adult faith formation program, it is no less true that the parish is an adult faith formation program" (*Our Hearts Were Burning Within Us*, 121).

1 Be responsive to the lives of adults—their unique life tasks, situations, needs, interests, and spiritual and faith journeys in the four distinct seasons of adulthood: young adults (20s–30s), midlife adults (40s–50s), mature adults (60s–70s), and older adults (80+).

Focusing on Young Adults

Adult catechesis with young adults is attentive to these key characteristics:

Identity exploration and self-discovery: trying out various possibilities, especially in love and work, and developing an individual sense of autonomy.

Significant transitions: leaving home/home ownership, getting married and starting a family, climbing the career ladder, taking on leadership roles, and achieving professional goals.

Autonomy: prioritizing the pursuit of their own goals and dreams.

Stress: adjusting to the expectations and responsibilities of the "adult" world.

Risk-taking: exploring new opportunities or exciting activities or making daring decisions.

Global awareness: valuing multiculturalism, global cooperation, and different perspectives.

Equality and inclusion: advocating for the rights of marginalized groups and supporting initiatives that address climate change.

Spiritual but not religious (as well as the Nones): expressing a sense of spirituality and belief in God but not identifying with or belonging to an organized religion.

Question traditional beliefs: seeking a deeper understanding of their own beliefs, exploring other faith traditions, or critically examining the tenets of their upbringing.

Spiritually hungry: being drawn to a faith that aligns with their values and resonates with their experiences instead of adhering strictly to beliefs of their childhood.

Focusing on Midlife Adults

Adult catechesis with midlife adults is attentive to these key characteristics:

Reevaluation: reassessing identity, life purposes and goals, values, and hopes for the future.

Diverse perspectives: flowing from their wealth of life experiences at work and in the world.

Transitions: experiencing parent transitions (empty nesters, parenting teenagers and/or navigating blended families), grandparenting, caregiving for aging parents, death of parents, and more.

A pragmatic approach to life: having significant responsibilities in life leads to a more a practical approach to problem-solving and decision-making.

Life changes (career, family, life circumstances): leading to the necessity for coping strategies, emotional intelligence, and self-care.

Leisure activities: desiring to make time for activities that bring fulfillment and joy.

"Midlife crisis": experiencing a time of discontent, followed by self-reflection, questioning, and a desire for change.

Responsible citizenship: desiring to make positive contributions to society.

Religious diversity: being tolerant and welcoming of many beliefs and practices.

Faith and spirituality: confronting questions about the meaning and purpose of life, leading to a deepened exploration of the spiritual aspects of life.

Focusing on Mature Adults

Adult catechesis with mature adults is attentive to these key characteristics:

Life reassessment: taking time to reassess a new stage of life without parenting or full-time work; exploring the question "Who am I now?"

Legacy: desiring to create or nurture things that will outlast themselves.

Retirement: making the transition from full-time work often involves life reinvention, dealing with loss of a sense of identity because of retirement.

Health: managing overall well-being and dealing with new physical limitations and health conditions.

Life planning: addressing legal matters, including creating or updating wills, advance directives, and powers of attorney.

Continued learning: engaging in a variety of personal learning projects and continued intellectual growth.

New interests: Cultivating new cultural interests, hobbies, interest in music and drama performances, travel and leisure activities, and more.

Grief: experiencing the death of friends, spouses, or family members.

Faith: finding faith and spirituality a source of comfort and deeper meaning in later life.

Spirituality: seeking reflective spiritual practices.

Focusing on Older Adults

Adult catechesis with older adults is attentive to these key characteristics:

Independence and autonomy: desiring to retain the ability to make decisions about their lives.

Housing transitions: experiencing downsizing, modifying homes for aging in place, exploring assisted living or senior communities or nursing homes, and more.

Health challenges: experiencing mobility issues, declining physical ability (loss of hearing, vision, or dexterity), and the potential for cognitive decline.

Well-being: maintaining overall well-being, accessing medical care, and managing chronic conditions.

Connections: seeking out friendships, community involvement, and/or family interactions.

Wisdom: having the opportunity to share life stories and insights with others, including the experience of living through wars, technological advancements, social movements, and economic transformations.

Rediscovering purpose: exploring new ways to live a life of meaning in older adulthood.

Dying and death: dealing with questions such as "What is life about?" and "How do I want to die?"

Deepening spirituality: growing into a deeper, more personal faith.

Spiritual exploration: being open to new ideas often leads to a shift in emphasis on certain aspects of faith or a more personalized and eclectic approach to spirituality.

*See Practice Resource #13: Characteristics of the Seasons of Adulthood for a more detailed description of each stage of adulthood at **ncclcatholic.org/ guided-by-the-directory***.

2 Incorporate the ways that adults learn best into all catechetical programming and experiences.

Adults learn best through a combination of strategies that consider their unique characteristics, experiences, and preferences. The following strategies apply to all adults, but each strategy needs to be adapted for each stage of adulthood: young adults (20s–30s), midlife adults (40s–50s), mature adults (60s–70s), and older adults (80+). Some strategies may apply more appropriately to one or two sea-

sons of adulthood, such as digital technology with young adults.

Active participation: Adults learn best when they actively engage with the learning material rather than passively receiving information. This can include hands-on activities, discussions, problem-solving exercises, and interactive learning experiences.

Relevant and meaningful content: Adult learners are motivated when they can see the immediate relevance and practical applications of what they are learning. Content that aligns with their personal goals and addresses real-life challenges is more likely to resonate with them.

Prior knowledge integration: Building on adults' existing knowledge and experiences can enhance learning. Relating new information to what they already know helps them make connections and better understand complex concepts.

Self-directed learning: Adults value autonomy and prefer to take control of their learning process. Allowing them to set their own learning goals, choose learning activities, and take responsibility for their progress fosters a sense of ownership and motivation.

Collaborative learning: Group interactions and collaborative activities provide opportunities for adult learners to share ideas, perspectives, and experiences. Learning from peers and engaging in discussions can deepen understanding and critical thinking.

Reflection and feedback: Providing opportunities for adults to reflect on what they've learned and receive timely feedback on their performance helps reinforce learning and identify areas for improvement.

Practical application: Adult learners benefit from opportunities to apply their newly acquired knowledge or skills in real-life situations. Practical application enhances retention and transfer of learning to their personal or professional contexts.

Flexibility and personalized learning: Adults have diverse needs and preferences. Offering flexible learning options and personalized pathways accommodates different learning styles and individual schedules.

Experiential learning: Learning through hands-on experiences and real-life situations is particularly effective for adults.

Multimedia and technology: Utilize multimedia and technology to enhance the learning experience. Incorporate videos, interactive modules, online discussions, and virtual simulations to cater to different learning styles and preferences.

Emotion and memory: Emotional experiences can significantly impact memory and learning retention. Designing learning experiences that evoke positive emotions and meaningful connections can enhance the learning process.

Positive learning environment: Creating a positive and supportive learning environment fosters motivation and engagement. Encouragement, positive reinforcement, and recognition of learners' achievements contribute to a conducive learning atmosphere.

Flexibility: Adult learners have busy lives and diverse responsibilities. Providing flexible learning options allows them to balance learning with other commitments.

Lifelong learning: Adults continue to learn throughout their lives. Recognizing the importance of lifelong learning and promoting a growth mindset encourages adults to seek ongoing opportunities for skill development and personal growth.

*See Practice Resource #14: Learning Strategies for the Generations of Adulthood for a more detailed description of each stage of adulthood at **ncclcatholic.org/ guided-by-the-directory***.

3 Provide a holistic formation in faith for each season of adulthood–young adults, midlife adults, mature adults, and older adults–with a rich menu of faith-forming experiences each year that are responsive to the diverse spiritual-religious lives of adults. Guide adults in discerning where they are in their faith journey, charting a path for faith growth, and providing programming and experiences tailored to their lives.

Adult catechesis can guide adults in discerning where they are in their faith journey and charting a path for faith growth that helps them get from where they are in their faith journey to a deeper relationship with Jesus and practice of the faith. People should be able to clearly understand where they are in their faith journey and their next steps in faith growth. (See "Adult Faith Approaches" in paragraph 258 in the *Directory*.)

Catechesis can provide programming and experiences specifically designed for:

Adults who have a vibrant faith and relationship with God and are engaged in a faith community: nourishing their faith through a variety of faith-forming experiences to promote their deeper growth, such as engaging in Bible study, study of theology, or spiritual formation; equipping adults to share and witness their faith; and offering a variety of activities that help them grow deeper in their faith.

Adults who participate occasionally in the faith community and whose faith is less central to their daily lives: inviting them into a supportive *community* where they can build relationships with other adults and experience a sense of belonging to the parish community; inviting them into experiences that refresh their faith (study of Jesus, the Gospels, prayer); exploring how to make a relationship with Jesus Christ more central to their daily life; and offering a variety of activities that help them to engage in the community and live their faith.

Adults who are uninvolved in a faith community and who value and live their spirituality outside of organized religion: seeking out the uninvolved and inviting them into safe spaces and small groups to explore a new relationship with Jesus Christ and what following him could mean for their life; hearing the Good News (again or for the first time) and what it means for life today; inviting them into experiences of faith in action in the parish community: serving those in need, praying, working for justice, worshipping; offering a variety of activities to encounter Jesus Christ and his community in new and fresh ways.

Adults who are unaffiliated and have left involvement in organized religion and have little need for God in their lives: connecting with the unaffiliated in the wider community and inviting them into safe spaces to explore how one lives with meaning and purpose today; to discern how religion might provide support for living a meaningful life; to uncover the wisdom in the Christian tradition that could guide their life; to test out a relationship with Jesus Christ; to see how the Good News might be good news for them.

A menu of faith-forming experiences can be tailored to the profiles of adult faith and practice. A menu approach provides a way to structure learning with experiences, programs, and activities designed to promote growth in faith for adults who want to grow deeper in the faith, for those who are inquiring or aren't sure the Christian faith is for them, and for those who don't need God or religion in their lives.

A menu of adult catechesis can be built around the *five tasks of catechesis*: knowledge of the faith, celebration of the mystery (liturgies and seasons of the liturgical year), forming for life in Christ (moral life), prayer, and active engagement in community life.

Adults could select from a menu of *life stage*–appropriate catechesis around the unique life tasks, needs, interests, and spiritual and faith journeys of young adults (20s–30s), midlife adults (40s–50s), mature adults (60s–70s), and older adults (80+).

A menu approach has 1) a variety of content, programs, activities, and resources; 2) a variety of formats—on your own, mentored, small groups, and large groups; 3) a variety of times to participate and scheduling options (synchronous and asynchronous); and 4) hybrid, online, and gathered modes of programming.

The menu approach puts adults at the center of catechesis and gives them choice over what and when and where they will learn. It moves away from one-size-fits-all catechesis for adults. It provides the opportunity for variety, choice, and personalization.

The movement from one-size-fits-all catechesis to a variety of faith formation offerings for each season of adulthood is made possible by the abundance of religious content and programming—print, audio, video, online, and digital—that is now available. This abundance can now be made accessible to people by the creation of online platforms (websites and social media) and digital playlists that integrate, deliver, and communicate the content and programming with a variety of ways to learn that is easily available, anytime and anywhere.

 See Practice 7 in chapter 2 for more information on programming.

An Example
What if we offered adult faith formation tailored to the adult faith profiles?

1. "Taste and see" experiences
2. "Refresher" experiences
3. "Growing" experiences
4. "Going deeper" experiences

Scripture Study Focused on the New Lectionary Cycle

Introduction to the Gospel

- Online two-part video-based introduction using videos from The Bible Project (**https://bibleproject.com**)
- Podcasts and audio programming on the Gospel

Exploration of the Gospel (four sessions)
Four-week speaker series: Overview of Gospel, Teachings of Jesus, Ministry of Jesus, and Passion-Resurrection

- Gathered format at church (morning and evening sessions)
- Streamed live online
- Recorded for viewing on YouTube
- Offered as a four-session small-group format with videos and study guide

Growing and Going Deeper through Bible Study
Six-session Bible study of the Gospel

- At church with morning and evening sessions for small groups
- Small groups in homes or other setting
- Online small groups using Zoom
- On-your-own learning

Going Deeper through an Online Gospel Course
Eight-session online course for on-your-own learning or small-group learning

Curated On-Your-Own Resources

- Bible websites
- Online Bible apps
- Books and video programs

Programming Tools
(Available at **ncclcatholic.org/guided-by-the-directory**)

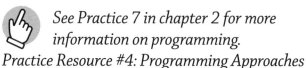 *See Practice 7 in chapter 2 for more information on programming. Practice Resource #4: Programming Approaches for Catechesis, Practice Resource #5: Using Contemporary Methods for Catechesis, Practice Resource #6: Using Digital Methods in Catechesis.*

4 Adult catechesis provides adults with multiple ways to experience one program.

With multiple ways to design programming in physical, online, and hybrid spaces, one program or experience can be designed in all three spaces, increasing the availability to a wider audience of people. The choice is no longer whether to participate but which option best suits a person's time, schedule, and learning preferences. Here is an example of a large-group program that is redesigned for multiple formats—same program, multiple ways to experience it.

Large-group physical gathering: Adults gather at church for a live presentation or to watch a video presentation with leader(s) to facilitate the program: providing time for people to read and reflect, guiding small groups in discussing the content, etc. The live presentation is video recorded for use in other settings.

Small-group physical gathering: Adults gather in small groups in homes or coffee shops or another conducive setting, watch the video, read and reflect on the content, and discuss the content.

Small-group hybrid: Adults view the video on their own and then gather online in a small group (Zoom or other video conferencing platform) to reflect and discuss the content.

Online with interaction: Adults complete the sessions on their own and share reflections in a Facebook group (asynchronous) or meet on Zoom to discuss the program (synchronous).

Online independent: Adults complete the learning program on their own.

The "one program, multiple models" approach can dramatically increase catechetical offerings and give control to adults so they can choose what and when and how and where they will learn.

5 Expand the opportunities to engage more adults in learning and faith growth with "on-your-own" faith-forming experiences.

According to the AARP research report "Lifelong Learning Among 45+ Adults" (**aarp.org/research/ topics/life/info-2022/lifelong-learning-older-adults.html**), adults 45+ often see lifelong learning as a self-directed, individual activity. The majority choose to read or gather information by themselves and then find opportunities to apply what they have learned in real life. Expanding *On Your Own formats*

provides maximum flexibility for the learner—when to learn, how to learn, where to learn, and what to learn. With the increasing number and variety of books and printed resources, audio podcasts, video presentations, video programs, online courses, and online resource centers, independent learning offers a 24/7 approach to faith growth and learning. Churches can serve as a guide to help people find the best learning format and content to address their learning needs.

Churches can develop fully online programming (asynchronous) by offering independent (on-your-own) faith formation using the abundance of online programs and resources for adults. Leaders can curate courses and resources to organize playlists or web pages with self-directed learning topics like Scripture, topics in Catholic theology, prayer and spiritual formation, social justice issues, morality and ethics, and much more.

*See Practice Resource #6: Using Digital Methods in Catechesis for digital strategies to use in adult catechesis at **ncclcatholic.org/guided-by-the-directory**.*

6 Provide interest-centered small groups on a variety of topics that integrate faith and life around the interests and gifts of adults in each season of adulthood.

Small-group formats provide lots of flexibility in content, schedule, and location (in physical settings, online settings, or hybrid settings). Groups can meet at times and places that best fit people's lives. They can have short commitments to make it easier for adults to participate. Interest-centered groups can draw upon a wide range of gifts and talents from adults. Small groups can be developed around a variety of topics—each one connecting life and faith. Each small group can include a teaching component, along with practice, and performance components. Here are several examples:

Life-centered: times of transition, life issues in each season of adulthood

Creative: art, music, drama, and more

Spiritual: how to pray, spiritual practices, spiritual direction, and more

Biblical: what's in the Bible, how to read and interpret the Bible, big questions in the Bible, and more

Action: serving people in need, responding to justice issues, caring for creation

Leadership: involvement in leadership roles in church and the community

Theological: what does Jesus mean for our life today, living as a disciple, living morally, and more

7 Address the many transitions of adulthood.

Adulthood is filled with transitions: geographic relocations, family formation and re-formation, career changes, empty nests, unanticipated illness, and the loss of loved ones. In times of transition, most people experience feelings of disorientation and tend to question personal priorities; they may seek to "finish unfinished business" or develop new dimensions of their lives. Adults seek to acquire new meaning perspectives and frameworks that can help them regain order and stability in their lives.

Addressing the needs of people in transition provides important opportunities for adult faith formation by bringing a faith perspective to the transitions adults are experiencing. Recognize that these transitions may prompt a hunger for learning and provide learning opportunities that are responsive to immediate concerns. Their new learning may lead them to new questioning and unanticipated changes in the views of self and world.

Catechesis can target adults who are experiencing transition and change and offer to help them chart a course of learning that can help them find meaning in their lives. Fashion catechesis around the times of transitions and change in the lives of adults with learning, ritual, prayer, and community support. Here are just a few examples of transition times: graduating college, going into the military (and returning home from military service), starting a new job or losing a job, getting married, becoming a parent, becoming a grandparent, becoming an empty nest family, retiring, surviving a major illness/accident, becoming a caregiver, experiencing the loss of a loved one, and much more.

8 Engage adults in exploring their Christian vocation and how God calls them throughout the seasons of adulthood— as young adults, midlife adults, mature adults, and older adults.

Vocation is a central part of the Christian life, encompassing *who we are called to be*, *how we are called to live*, and *what we are called to do*. Vocation relates to our whole life and encompasses a multiplicity of callings. Vocation is not limited to one part of life or one kind of work or one lifestyle. It is a dynamic reality that changes throughout our life, not something determined at the outset. Vocation is a lifelong reality. Each season of adulthood brings new challenges and possibilities: How do our callings change as we grow? What does it mean that God calls us in relationship to the whole of our lives (including our work, relationships, and identity)— all life long?

We are called by God, who is the source of our callings. We are called to follow the way shown by Jesus and taken up by his disciples—this calling we share with each other. We are called as unique persons with a particular history and circumstance. We are called from the losses and grief we suffer over time so that we can embrace life again. We are called to give our lives to others, not simply for our self-improvement or fulfillment. We are even called in our deepest suffering to carry out God's purposes in mysterious ways. We are called through the people in our lives because vocation takes root in community. And, finally, we are called together to live within God's loving embrace, both now and in the life to come.

Develop vocation and calling programs for each stage of life (young adults, midlife adults, mature adults, and older adults) or around the major adult life transitions (entering adulthood, getting married, becoming a parent, retiring, etc.). Engage adults in discerning what their calling is at this time in their life and how to live their calling more fully in life. Offer a variety of programming options, such as a small-group experience for people at the same stage of life; a mentored (one-to-one) experience; a weekly, bi-weekly, or monthly course (in-person or hybrid); a retreat; and more.

9 Guide adults in developing a life of faith by exploring and experiencing the practices that constitute a Christian way of life, helping adults create their own "rule of life."

People come to faith and grow in faith and in the life of faith by participating in the practices of the Christian community. They learn the Christian way of life and its practices through experience and through guidance, mentoring, and teaching of other Christians who live these practices. Developing a Christian way of life and the practices that constitute that life is a process of developing skills, performing, thinking, and practicing repeatedly.

At the heart of Christian practice is Jesus: in his presence and example, a way to live comes into focus. We experience this model of living whenever we celebrate the blessings of life, serve the poor and vulnerable, offer our lives in prayer, forgive others, keep the Sabbath holy, discern God's will for us, or try to transform the world. Christian practices emerge repeatedly in the Bible and Christian tradi-

tion, and they have demonstrated their importance in forming a distinctively Christian way of life.

Adult catechesis that helps adults develop their way of living as Christians can include the following practices: caring for creation, discernment, doing justice, dying well, eating well, embracing diversity, finding God in everyday life, forgiveness, healing, honoring the body, hospitality, keeping Sabbath, praying, peace and reconciliation, reading the Bible, serving the poor and vulnerable, stewardship and generosity, and worship.

Engage adults in Christian practice learning programs through courses, workshops, retreats, action projects, and practice-focused small groups using a learning process that includes:

1. Preparing adults with the Scriptural and theological understanding of the practice

2. Engaging them in hands-on experience of the practice (with peers or intergenerationally)

3. Reflecting on the experience and its meaning for them

4. Integrating the practice into their daily lives

10 Move adult catechesis out to the wider community, expanding the locations for adult programming and experiences.

What if parishes focused on "bringing the church to people" in new spaces and locations, with programs and experiences that expand the scope and reach of the church into the lives of people in the neighborhood and community? What if parishes made a special effort to reach and engage people who are not involved or have given up on church or were never affiliated with any church or religion?

One approach is to move some of the at-church adult programs and activities into community settings, such as Bible study offered in community spaces like homes, coffee shops, or senior living centers. Changing the location of a program opens the possibility of inviting people to join in a neutral setting.

A second approach is to open up programs currently sponsored by the parish to the whole community, such as life-centered adult programs, service projects, or a speaker series.

A third approach is to offer activities directed to the needs and interests of people sponsored by the parish in a variety of community settings and spaces so that everyone feels comfortable participating. There have been examples of this type of outreach in the variety of Theology on Tap or God on Tap programs at neighborhood pubs. A church can offer a variety of programs and initiatives targeted to adults in general or to adults at particular stages in adulthood. Here are a few examples.

- Workshops, resources, and support groups targeted to the life tasks, transitions, and needs of each season of adulthood

- Dinner Church or Brunch Church experiences that bring people together over a meal to share stories, build relationships, find mutual support in life's struggles, and engage with each other spiritually

- Art and music workshops and courses, art exhibitions, music concerts, and drama performances

- Programs and activities designed for older adults at the senior center or adult living center or nursing home

- Career and life mentoring or coaching, especially for young adults

- Community-wide service days, service projects, and mission trips

- Organizing initiatives around social justice issues, both local and global

- Leadership training and engagement in leadership roles in the community

11 Utilize the catechumenal model of formation with sacramental preparation for adults and address their diverse spiritualities and faith practices.

See Practice 2 in chapter 2 for additional background on the catechumenal model of formation.

The catechumenal model of formation embodies all five interrelated tasks of catechesis in a holistic formation process that includes:

- A first proclamation of the Gospel (kerygma)

- A comprehensive introduction to the Christian life

- Liturgies, rituals, and symbols that engage the heart and the senses

- A community of faith and support

- Apprenticeship and mentoring in faith

- Engagement in the mission of the Church and service to the world

- Formation that fosters conversion of heart and mind in a new way of life

- Ever-deeper formation in faith and the life of the community (mystagogy)

Here are two examples of the catechumenal process applied to marriage preparation and adult confirmation.

The Catechumenal Model for Marriage Preparation

Catechumenal Pathways for Married Life (Vatican Dicastery of Laity, Family and Life, 2022) proposes a catechumenal model for marriage preparation:

The actual catechumenal phase consists of three distinct stages: proximate preparation, final preparation, and accompaniment during the first years of married life. In between the pre-catechumenal phase and the actual catechumenal phase, an intermediate phase may be envisaged in which the reception of candidates takes place, which could conclude with a ritual of entry into the marriage catechumenate... what follows is a bullet-point list of the various phases and stages, with some rituals and retreats delineating them:

Pre-catechumenal phase: remote preparation

- Youth ministry
- Young adult ministry

Intermediate phase (lasting a few weeks): period of reception of candidates

- Ritual of entry into the catechumenate (concluding the reception phase)

Catechumenal phase:

- First stage: proximate preparation (about a year)
  Rite of Betrothal (concluding the proximate preparation)
  Brief entrance retreat into final preparation
- Second stage: final preparation (a few months)
  Short retreat in preparation for wedding (a few days before the celebration)
- Third stage: first years of married life (two to three years)

The Catechumenal Model for Adult Confirmation

Using the catechumenal process, catechesis with adults can be *personalized* around their religious faith and practices today: 1) adults who have a vibrant faith and relationship with God and are engaged in a faith community; 2) adults who participate occasionally in the faith community and whose faith is less central to their daily lives; 3) adults who are uninvolved in a faith community and who value and live their spirituality outside of organized religion; and 4) adults who are unaffiliated, have left involvement in organized religion, and have little need for God or religion in their lives. The catechumenal process can offer catechesis for those who need "taste and see" experiences, "refresher" experiences, "growing" experiences, and "going deeper" experiences.

Three Pathways through Remote Preparation

- For adults who are not actively living their faith: provide a first proclamation of the Gospel (kerygma) and then an introduction to the Christian life. Consider offering a specialized mini-course or retreat experience or a small-group mentored experience focused on an introduction to the Christian faith and the parish community.
- For adults who are actively practicing their faith and have been involved in faith formation: provide a deeper exploration into the Bible and the Catholic tradition in areas of special interest to them.

PREPARATION

- Catechesis on the sacrament of Confirmation: theology, rituals, and symbols
- Engagement with a community of faith and support
- Retreat opportunities offered in different formats and time commitments
- Mentoring by members of the faith community

CELEBRATION OF THE SACRAMENT

CONTINUED GROWTH AND ACCOMPANIMENT (MYSTAGOGY)

- Continuing spiritual formation
- In-depth catechesis that is interest-based

- Exploration of calling and vocation
- Engagement in the faith community and involvement in parish ministries
- Ways to live one's faith in the community and world

Applying the Catechumenal Model to Adult Catechesis

The following reflective questions can guide your planning of adult faith formation:

- How does our catechesis for adults focus on conversion as a lifelong process?

- How can our catechesis for adults emphasize formation and transformation, rather than only information?

- How is our catechesis for adults gradual (rather than everything all at once)?

- How might our catechesis for adults involve and be nurtured within and by the whole community of faith?

- How does our adult catechesis programming respect and support the faith journeys of everyone?

- How are our adult catechesis and liturgy intimately connected?

- How is our catechesis for adults grounded in the word of God, presenting an appreciation of the mysteries of faith and an acquaintance with dogmas of the faith?

- How is our adult catechesis undergirded with the principle that all catechesis is welcoming and hospitable?

- How are prayer and spirituality deepened in all our catechetical processes for adults?

- Does our catechesis for adults enable faith-sharing?

- How is our catechesis for adults mystagogical?

- How is our catechesis for adults an apprenticeship for discipleship, an apprenticeship for living a Gospel life for others?

*See Practice Resource #15: Designing Programming Using the Catechumenal Model and Process for more specific questions and suggestions for practices flowing from each of these questions at **ncclcatholic.org/ guided-by-the-directory**.*

Conclusion

An important principle of adult catechesis is the necessity of responding to the needs and interests of our people. Consider:

- Is there a time and place for providing opportunities that parishioners haven't requested?

- Is it the role of leadership to raise awareness and consciousness, to invite people to go a little deeper, a little broader?

- Do we only provide spiritual enrichment (important as that is), or is our role also to challenge and provoke so that the Holy Spirit may transform us?

- Does your parish accommodate or challenge, enrich or transform?

- Do your parishioners need comfort or discomfort to deepen their commitment to God and one another?

- What topics/themes are people not asking for but need to live as disciples in today's world?

CHAPTER 6

PRACTICE RESOURCES

You will find the following Practice Resources at **ncclcatholic.org/ guided-by-the-directory:**

PRACTICE RESOURCE #13
Characteristics of the Seasons of Adulthood

PRACTICE RESOURCE #14
Learning Strategies for the Generations of Adulthood

PRACTICE RESOURCE #15
Designing Programming Using the Catechumenal Model and Process

The Christian
community
is a primary
agent of
catechesis

Catechesis with the Whole Community Together

PART 1. **Exploring the Vision of Catechesis for the Whole Community in the *Directory for Catechesis***

The Christian community is a primary agent of catechesis. "The faith is professed, celebrated, expressed, and lived above all in community: The communitarian dimension is not just a 'frame,' an 'outline,' but an integral part of the Christian life, of witness and of evangelization" (88).

In *Communities of Salt and Light* (1993), the U.S. bishops echo this understanding: "The parish is where the Church lives. Parishes are communities of faith, of action, and of hope. They are where the gospel is proclaimed and celebrated, where believers are formed and sent to renew the earth. Parishes are the home of the Christian community; they are the heart of our Church. Parishes are the place where God's people meet Jesus in word and sacrament and come in touch with the source of the Church's life."

The *Directory for Catechesis* presents the Christian community, the parish, as "the origin, locus, and goal of catechesis. Proclamation of the Gospel always begins with the Christian community and invites people to conversion and the following of Christ. It is the same community that welcomes those who wish to know the Lord better and permeate themselves with a new life" (133).

Catechesis with the whole community, i.e., intergenerational catechesis, engages all ages and generations and is situated within the life of the community. The *Directory* specifically mentions intergenerational catechesis in Chapter VIII in the "Catechesis and the Family" section.

> Intergenerational catechesis envisions the journey of faith as a formative experience not aimed at a particular age group but shared among different generations within a family or a community, on the pathway marked out by the liturgical year. This initiative makes the most of the exchange of the experience of faith among the generations, taking inspiration from the first Christian communities. (232)

Intergenerational catechesis helps parishes live the insight that the community is a primary agent of catechesis where faith is professed, celebrated, expressed, and lived with all ages and generations. Intergenerational catechesis models, approaches, and activities provide the parish with a way to engage all ages and generations together in learning, praying, serving, celebrating, and caring for each other. Specifically, intergenerational catechesis:

- Reclaims God's intent for faith to be shared in community and across generations and bring understanding and unity within a congregation.

- Creates a welcoming environment—hospitality, trust, acceptance, emotional safety, and care—conducive to promoting faith sharing, group participation, and mutual support across all generations.

- Strengthens relationships, connections, and community across generations, enhancing their sense of belonging to the faith community and increasing their participation in church life.

- Affirms each person's value in the total community, regardless of age, and utilizes the wisdom, experience, and knowledge of one generation to meet the needs of another generation.

- Teaches people to care for one another in the parish and in the community.

- Helps people learn the beliefs and practices of the Catholic faith as they participate with more experienced members of the parish community.

- Brings together the generations to learn from each other, share their faith stories, and support each other in practicing their faith in daily life.

- Develops the faith of all ages and generations as they engage together in sharing faith, learning, serving, celebrating, and praying with one another.

- Supports families by surrounding them with a community of faith and providing parents with opportunities to learn from practicing believers who have raised faithful children.

- Increases the opportunities for children and youth to have Christian role models outside of their families.

- Engages the creative gifts and talents of younger and older generations to serve the Church and world.

To learn more about the research on intergenerational faith formation, go to Practice Resource #16: Practices for Forming Faith Intergenerationally at **ncclcatholic.org/guided-by-the-directory**.

PART 2. Designing Catechesis for the Whole Community Inspired by the *Directory for Catechesis*

The five strategies proposed in this chapter are offered to stimulate your imagination and begin the process of envisioning new approaches for catechesis with the whole community—all ages and generations together. The five strategies include:

Strategy 1. Design catechesis around the intergenerational life and events of the parish community

Strategy 2. Transform multigenerational settings into intergenerational faith-forming experiences

Strategy 3. Redesign age-specific programs into intergenerational faith-forming experiences

Strategy 4. Create new intergenerational faith-forming initiatives

Strategy 5. Implement intergenerational learning models

STRATEGY 1. Design Catechesis around the Intergenerational Life and Events of the Parish Community

Building on the insight that the Christian community is a primary agent of catechesis where "the faith is professed, celebrated, expressed, and lived," intergenerational events and experiences of church life can serve as a primary content for catechesis with all ages. Parishes can build faith formation each year around the intergenerational events and experiences of church life, and then design intergenerational, family, and age-specific programming around the events. Here are several categories of church life events that can form the basis of a multi-year intergenerational curriculum.

- The feasts and seasons of the Church year provide a natural rhythm and calendar for fashioning faith: Advent and Christmas,

Epiphany, Baptism of the Lord, Call of the Disciples, Ash Wednesday, Lent, Holy Week, Easter, Easter season, Pentecost, feasts from ethnic traditions, and many more throughout the year.

- Sunday worship and the Lectionary readings provide a rich curriculum for the whole community with its cycle of weekly scripture readings.

- Rituals and sacramental celebrations provide events rich in theological meaning and faith practice that celebrate the faith journey throughout life.

- Acts of service and justice—locally and globally—provide a focus on mission to the world and put into action biblical and Church teaching on service, justice, and care for the earth.

- Prayer and spiritual traditions provide times for reflection, praying as a community, and living the practices of the spiritual life through the community's life together.

- Parish events that originate within the life and history of the community celebrate and reinforce the parish's identity and mission.

- Contemporary events in the lives of families, the community, and the world provide an opportunity for the church to respond to the signs of the times and how the Church and Christian faith can respond.

To unlock the faith-forming power of these events, design catechesis for all ages using this four-step methodology that guides people from preparing to experiencing to reflecting to living.

1. *Prepare*: provide formation programs— intergenerationally, in families, and/or

in age groups—that teach the knowledge and practices (biblical, theological) for participating in the event.

2. *Experience*: engage people in the direct experience of the event.

3. *Reflect*: guide people in reflecting on their experience of the event and its meaning for their lives.

4. *Live*: equip people with the practices, skills, and resources to integrate the meaning of the event into living as a Christian.

The methodology can be applied in a variety of ways. These examples illustrate the process:

Sunday Mass. *Prepare* people for Sunday worship and rehearse the Scripture readings. *Engage* them in the experience of Sunday worship and provide reflection activities. *Equip* them to live the Sunday worship experience at home and in their daily lives with activities and resources in print and digital formats.

Social justice. *Prepare* people on the biblical and Church teachings around a justice issue. *Engage* them in the experience/action to serve those in need or work for justice or care for creation—locally and globally. Provide reflection times and activities to connect action with faith. *Equip* them to live the practices of service, justice, and/or care for creation in their daily lives.

Scripture. *Prepare* people with the knowledge and skills to read, interpret, and apply the Bible to their lives. *Engage* them in experiencing and reflecting on the practices of reading the Bible at Sunday worship, through the seasons of the Church year, and in the life of the Church. *Equip* them to live their own practice of reading and studying the Bible.

Church year. *Prepare* people for exploring the life, teachings, death, and resurrection of Jesus through the seasons of the Church year. *Engage* them by experiencing the seasons of the Church year and reflecting on what they are learning about Jesus.

Equip them to live more fully as disciples of Jesus through their experience of the life, teachings, death, and resurrection of Jesus.

Prayer. *Prepare* people with the knowledge and practices for prayer and enriching their spiritual life. *Engage* them in a variety of experiences of prayer and spiritual practices in the life of the Church and opportunities for reflection on how to deepen their prayer and spiritual life. *Equip* them to develop their prayer life by living the practices of prayer and the spiritual disciplines in their daily lives.

STRATEGY 2. **Transform Multigenerational Settings into Intergenerational Faith-Forming Experiences**

Every parish has multigenerational environments in which at least two generations are participating in an event or activity—Sunday Mass, parish events and social gatherings, programs, and classes. Parishes can utilize these environments to connect generations through relationship building and shared experiences.

How can your church transform multigenerational environments into experiences of intergenerational connection and community? List all of the parish's multigenerational events and activities. Take one example and apply the following questions to it.

- *Consider relationships*: How will the generations interact with each other, get to know each other, share stories with each other? How will the experience incorporate intentional relationship-building activities? How will everyone feel welcomed and safe?

- *Consider the content*: How will the experience engage generations in shared activities and in generationally appropriate activities?

- *Consider prayer*: How will the prayer or prayer experience engage all generations? What prayer forms and activities are best suited for an all-ages group?

- *Consider leadership*: How will each generation be involved in leadership roles that are appropriate to their gifts, abilities, and age? How will the leadership team engage multiple generations?

- *Consider inclusion*: How will each generation feel valued and recognized in the experience?

- *Consider communication*: How will communication and social media channels be inclusive of all generations and provide connection among the generations?

STRATEGY 3. **Redesign Age-Specific Programs into Intergenerational Faith-Forming Experiences**

Age-specific programs and activities can provide opportunities for intergenerational connection, relationship building, and shared experiences. Opportunities abound in children and youth programming, Vacation Bible School, service and mission trips, retreats, Bible studies, and more.

How can you transform age-specific programs by adding intergenerational activities or by redesigning the program into an intergenerational experience?

- *Consider adding intergenerational activities*: How can your church incorporate another generation in sharing their faith, wisdom, and interests in the program (interviews, storytelling, presentations, demonstrations)? How can you add mentors or spiritual guides to a program (such as grandparent mentors for young parents or spiritual guides for young people preparing for Confirmation)?

- *Consider replacing age-specific with intergenerational throughout the year*: How can your church incorporate regular intergenerational gatherings into your age-group programs throughout the year?

- *Consider redesigning the program*: How can your church redesign an age-specific program into an intergenerational program involving at least one additional generation, such as transforming camp or Vacation Bible School (VBS) into a grandparent-grandchild program or transforming a youth service program or mission trip into an intergenerational service activity for all ages? Here are several ideas that illustrate how to transform age-specific programming into intergenerational opportunities:

  - Include all generations in Sunday Mass and involve all generations in leadership roles—music, art, hospitality, reading Scripture, and more.

  - Add other generations into current age-group programs, such as mission trips, service projects, retreat experiences, and VBS. Consider adding intergenerational experiences into VBS, such as a grandparent component or redesigning the youth mission trip into an all-ages mission trip.

  - Incorporate intergenerational dialogues, interviews, and presentations into programming, providing opportunities for children and youth to experience the wisdom, faith, and interests of (older) adults; and then reverse the process and provide opportunities for the (older) adults to experience the wisdom, faith, and interests of children or teens through presentations, performances, and discussions.

  - Add a mentoring component into programming for children, adolescents, and parents: parent mentors for baptismal parents, Confirmation mentors, learning-to-pray mentors, justice and service mentors, to name a few possibilities.

- Connect people of different generations who have insights and life experiences that may be helpful to other generations, such as midlife and mature adults helping new parents with financial management and household management, or young people helping older adults navigate the digital and online world.

- Add intergenerational relationship building and activities into social and recreational activities in the church community, such as the church picnic and after-worship gatherings.

STRATEGY 4. **Create New Intergenerational Faith-Forming Initiatives**

The last two strategies focus on redesigning; Strategy 4 involves designing new intergenerational initiatives (programs, activities, resources). This is an opportunity to create new programs, activities, or experiences that bring together all the generations for learning, celebrating, praying, reading the Bible, serving and working for justice, worshipping, and more. Consider designing a new intergenerational Vacation Bible School, summer camp, service projects and mission trips, retreat experiences, field trips, as well as grandparent and grandchild programming.

Where are the greatest needs and/or opportunities for creating new intergenerational initiatives that bring generations together?

STRATEGY 5. **Implement Intergenerational Learning Models**

Intergenerational learning provides a way to educate the whole community, bringing all ages and generations together to learn with and from each other, build community, share faith, pray, celebrate, and practice the Christian faith. The key is that everyone is learning together—young and old, single and married, families with children and empty nesters—and it involves the whole family—children, parents, grandparents—in a shared experience of the Christian faith. Parishes can make intergenerational learning central to lifelong faith formation in at least two ways: as their core faith formation program for all ages, supplemented by age-specific and age-group catechetical programs, or as one element in catechetical programming with age groups.

In the *first approach*, churches make intergenerational learning their core catechetical experience for all ages, conducting monthly, biweekly, or weekly intergenerational programs and then offering a variety of age-group or peer group programs throughout the month or year to address specific age-appropriate needs. These churches replace or modify their age-group programming to place the emphasis on all ages learning together. They often develop a multi-year curriculum for the whole community that can be built around themes from the Bible, the cycle of Sunday Lectionary readings, Church year feasts and seasons, Christian practices, service and social justice, prayer and spiritual disciplines, core Christian beliefs, and moral teachings.

In the *second approach*, churches implement intergenerational learning in targeted ways, such as adding an all-ages activity after Sunday worship, integrating an intergenerational component into Vacation Bible School, preparing for a sacrament or milestone celebration, learning about an upcoming Church year feast or season (Advent–Christmas, Lent, Holy Week, Easter, Pentecost), or replacing an age-group program with intergenerational learning on the same theme, to name a few examples.

Intergenerational learning incorporates three essential elements: all-ages learning, in-depth learning in one of three formats, and sharing learning and applying the learning to life. Intergenerational learning programs are extended-time programs and incorporate the following program elements:

1. A shared meal

2. A shared prayer experience

3. An *all-ages learning* experience on the topic of the program, with content and methods appropriate for an all-ages audience

4. *In-depth learning* on the topic, exploring the content of the program in age-appropriate ways. In-depth learning can be conducted in three different ways:

   - *Whole-group format* provides a series of facilitated learning activities for all ages together—in intergenerational groups or family/age groups—with activities appropriate to each group.

   - *Age-group format* provides parallel, age-appropriate learning for groups at the same time, with content and learning activities appropriate for each age group—children, young people, adults, and family or parent groups.

   - *Activity center learning* provides structured activities for all ages as well as age-specific learning activities to explore and experience the content of the program.

5. An *integration activity* for all ages to discover how to apply their learning to daily life using resources and activities provided in print or digital formats.

Use Practice Resource #17: Intergenerational Learning Design Worksheet as a guide for designing an intergenerational session at **ncclcatholic.org/ guided-by-the-directory**.

Examples of Intergenerational Catechesis as the Primary Model of Catechesis

Intergenerational catechesis as the primary learning model for all ages is developed around monthly or yearly themes drawn from the Creed, sacraments, morality, justice and service, prayer and spiritual life, Church year seasons, Scripture, Christian practices, and more.

Intergenerational learning models blend gathered experiences (at church or in small groups), at-home faith formation, and online resources. They can be structured and scheduled in several ways to respond to the needs of a parish community, such as monthly, twice monthly, or weekly programming. Here are a few examples:

Monthly Plan

WEEK #1. Intergenerational session at church or in small groups (1.5 to 2 hours)

WEEK #2. At-home faith formation with online resources

WEEK #3. At-home faith formation with online resources

WEEK #4. At-home faith formation with online resources

Monthly Plan with Age-Group Learning

WEEK #1. Intergenerational session at church or in small groups (1.5 to 2 hours)

WEEK #2. At-home faith formation with online resources

WEEK #3. Age-group learning session at church (1.5 hours)

WEEK #4. At-home faith formation with online resources

Twice-Monthly Plan

WEEK #1. Intergenerational session at church or in small groups (1.5 to 2 hours)

WEEK #2. At-home faith formation with online resources

WEEK #3. Intergenerational session at church or in small groups (1.5 to 2 hours)

WEEK #4. At-home faith formation with online resources

Weekly Plan

In the Weekly Plan, the movements of the intergenerational learning process are assigned to individual weeks. Over a month, the entire learning process is experienced. Each session is usually one hour in length.

WEEK #1. An all-ages learning experience, with content and methods appropriate to all ages

WEEK #2. An in-depth learning conducted in one of three ways: a) whole community learning together, with all ages and age-appropriate activities; b) parallel groups (children, teens, adults, parents) learning at the same time, with content and learning activities appropriate to each age group; and c) learning activity centers for all ages and for specific age groups

WEEK #3. An activity to help all ages discover how to apply their learning to daily life using resources and activities provided in print or digital formats

WEEK #4. At-home practice with online resources

CHAPTER 7
PRACTICE RESOURCES

You will find the following Practice Resources at **ncclcatholic.org/ guided-by-the-directory**:

PRACTICE RESOURCE #16
Practices for Forming Faith Intergenerationally

PRACTICE RESOURCE #17
Intergenerational Learning Design Worksheet

Designing New Catechetical Initiatives in the Parish

To be a designer is to be a steward of possibility. We search for outcomes that do not yet exist and in doing so we dive deep into the unexpected and unknown. (STANFORD SCHOOL OF DESIGN, HTTPS://DLIBRARY.STANFORD.EDU)

What could it look like if we designed catechesis for families and each stage of life that was guided by the vision and practices in the *Directory for Catechesis*?

The vision and practices in the *Directory for Catechesis* and the new context of catechesis today call for designing adaptive responses—new ways of thinking and acting—that create new catechetical approaches, programs, activities, and resources. Adaptive responses are flexible and dynamic responses to changing circumstances, involving the ability to learn, innovate, and adjust behaviors or strategies to effectively address new challenges or situations.

To assist you in developing new initiatives in parish catechesis inspired by the *Directory for Catechesis*, we are proposing a modified version of the design process created by the Stanford School of Design, which includes five modes of design thinking: *empathize*, *define*, *ideate*, *prototype*, and *test*. We have added a step to the process to help you *connect* your design work to the *Directory for Catechesis*.

1. Empathize with your target audience.

2. Define the design challenge from the perspective of your target audience.

3. Connect to the *Directory for Catechesis* for vision and practices.

4. Generate ideas and strategies for addressing the design challenge, inspired by the *Directory*.

5. Create prototypes (experiences, programs, activities, resources) that use the new strategies and can be tested with the target audience.

6. Test the prototypes with the target audience, obtain feedback from the target audience, and make revisions. Then offer the new initiative to a wider audience.

This chapter outlines a process you and your team can use to design new catechetical projects.

*For a complete guide with tools and worksheets, use Practice Resource #18: Guide for Designing New Catechetical Initiatives at **ncclcatholic.org/guided-by-the-directory***.

The Design Process

Identify Your Target Audience
Who are you designing for? Be as specific as possible.

Step 1. Develop Methods to Empathize with Your Target Audience
How can we develop an understanding of the people we are designing for?

Good design is grounded in a deep understanding of the people for whom you are designing. To understand more deeply the lives of your target audience, use your listening methods to discover:

- the life situations of your target audience
- the life tasks specific to their stage(s) of life
- their interests, concerns, needs, and questions
- their religious and spiritual characteristics

Develop one or more strategies to develop understanding of your target audience: listening sessions (focus groups), short surveys, interviews, and observation.

*Use Practice Resource #19: Tools for Understanding Your Audience with sample surveys and a guide to conduct focus groups and interviews at **ncclcatholic.org/ guided-by-the-directory***.

An *Empathy Map* (see following page) is a good tool to help you synthesize your findings and observations from your listening strategies and draw out unexpected insights. Use this tool with your planning team and key leaders. Use one large newsprint sheet or one sheet for each quadrant: Say, Do, Think,

Feel. Have everyone add their ideas directly on the newsprint sheets or on Post-it notes that are then posted into the four quadrants. When everyone is done, reflect together on your Empathy Map: identify the insights that surfaced and the needs you can discern.

Step 2. Define the Challenge
What is the design challenge you want to address in developing catechesis with your target audience?

The define mode is when you unpack and synthesize your empathy findings into compelling needs and insights, and then develop a specific and meaningful challenge. The key task is to come up with an actionable challenge to address in the lives of your target audience. Here are a few examples:

Adults: How can we engage adults in faith-forming experiences that address their complex lives, busy schedules, and diverse religious and spiritual needs?

Parents: How can we help parents feel more confident and capable in raising their young children today?

Young people: How can we involve younger generations in catechetical experiences that engage them (head, heart, hands) and are designed around how they learn best today?

*Step 3. Connect to the **Directory for Catechesis***
What can you draw upon from the *Directory for Catechesis* to address your design challenge, especially the vision and practices described in the *Directory* for your target audience?

Explore the key practices from the *Directory* by reviewing Chapter Two: Shaping the Catechetical Practices of the Parish, which includes:

- religious-spiritual lives of people today
- model and process of the baptismal catechumenal

Empathy Map

SAY

What are people saying about their lives, faith, spirituality, etc.?

DO

What are people doing or how are they living?

What do you notice about their actions and behaviors?

SAY

What are people thinking: What are their convictions, beliefs?

What do they value and find important in life?

FEEL

What are they feeling?

What emotions might they have?

- three faith-forming environments: intergenerational community, three-generational family, and age groups
- catechetical approaches for the uniqueness of each culture in the parish
- culture of full inclusion and catechetical programming for persons with disabilities

- human experience as integral to catechesis
- processes and methods for educating and forming people in the faith
- digital tools and approaches

Review the vision and strategies presented in this book for your target audience. Highlight strategies that are especially relevant to your design challenge.

Step 4. Generate Ideas and Strategies

What strategies can address the design challenge and reflect the vision and practices of the *Directory for Catechesis*?

The key in generating ideas or strategies is to give yourself and the team the freedom to imagine the possibilities. To do this, try to follow these simple rules:

- Generate as many ideas and strategies as possible to address the design challenge.
- Assume you have the resources you need for any idea (money, staff, facility, etc.).
- Don't place limits on your creativity.
- Remind people that there will be no discussion and no critique of ideas.
- Feel free to add on to others' ideas.

You may find it helpful to use a focusing question such as: *What would it be like if we…*

List the ideas on paper or electronically.

After you have finished generating strategies, connect similar ideas into one strategy. Then create a final list of all the ideas you have generated.

Step 5. Create Prototypes

How can you transform your ideas and strategies into projects/initiatives that your target audience can experience?

Review your list of strategies. Discuss which strategies would be most effective in addressing the design challenge. Highlight the strategies that you would like to move from idea to design. Then select

one or more that you want to use to create prototypes (projects).

Prototyping is translating the strategy you selected into experiences, programs, activities, and resources that you can test with your target audience. Use these questions to guide your design work:

Goal: What do we want to accomplish?

Strategies/activities: How will we accomplish the goal?

Personnel: Who will lead and implement the project?

Resources: What resources are needed to implement the project?

Timing: What is the timeframe for implementing the project?

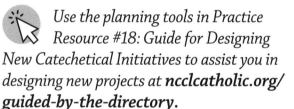 *Use the planning tools in Practice Resource #18: Guide for Designing New Catechetical Initiatives to assist you in designing new projects at **ncclcatholic.org/ guided-by-the-directory**.*

See the two examples at the end of this chapter that illustrate the design process.

Step 6. Test the Prototypes

How can you pilot the new project or initiative, obtain feedback on people's experience, and revise the design?

Identify a group within the target audience to pilot (test) the project. Implement the project and get regular feedback on its implementation and effectiveness. Develop leaders through the piloting phase so they can be involved in the wider launch of the project.

Testing is the chance to get feedback on your project, refine the project to make it better, and continue to learn about your audience. Testing is another opportunity to build empathy through observation and engagement. It often yields unexpected insights that can shape your redesign and improvement of the project.

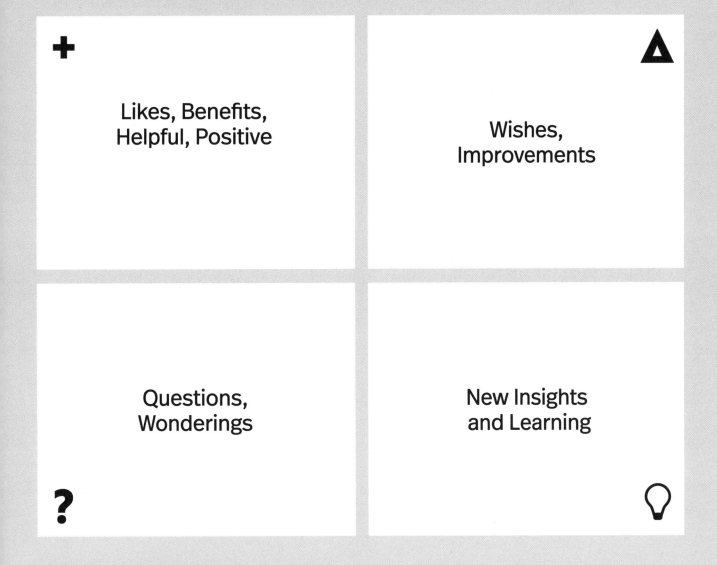 *Review the evaluation tools in Practice Resource #18: Guide for Designing New Catechetical Initiatives at **ncclcatholic.org/ guided-by-the-directory**.*

Use a *Feedback Capture Grid* (see below) to facilitate feedback from the participants about their experi-ence of the project. The grid helps you be systematic about feedback and more intentional about captur-ing thoughts in the four different areas.

Gather the participants in the project (or conduct focus groups or a short survey/evaluation) with the four questions of the Feedback Capture Grid.

Create the grid on a sheet of newsprint or on four sheets—one for each question. Draw a plus in the upper left quadrant, a delta in the upper right quad-rant, a question mark in the lower left quadrant, and

Feedback Capture Grid

+

Likes, Benefits, Helpful, Positive

Δ

Wishes, Improvements

?

Questions, Wonderings

New Insights and Learning

a light bulb in the lower right quadrant. Things one likes or finds notable are placed in the upper left; constructive criticism goes in the upper right; questions that the experience raised go in the lower left; ideas that the experience or presentation spurred go in the lower right.

For an in-person evaluation: Engage people in writing responses into the four quadrants (or writing on Post-it notes and then posting their note in the appropriate quadrant). For a summary of evaluations, fill the four quadrants with people's feedback.

Review and analyze the findings. What did you discover? Determine what was most effective, what needs to be changed, what needs to be eliminated.

Use the feedback to develop the second version of the design you want to offer to a wider audience.

Use the Feedback Capture Grid at the conclusion of the project.

CHAPTER 8
PRACTICE RESOURCES

You will find the following Practice Resources at **ncclcatholic.org/ guided-by-the-directory:**

PRACTICE RESOURCE #18
Guide for Designing New Catechetical Initiatives

PRACTICE RESOURCE #19
Tools for Understanding Your Audience

GUIDED BY THE DIRECTORY FOR CATECHESIS

From Design Challenge to Prototype

Adults in the Midlife and Mature Years

Target Audience
Two adult seasons: midlife (40s–50s) and mature (60s–70s)

Design Challenge
How can we engage adults in faith-forming experiences that address their complex lives, busy schedules, and diverse religious and spiritual needs?

*Connect to the **Directory for Catechesis***
The relationship of adults with the question of faith is highly varied, and it is right that every person should be welcome and listened to in his(her) uniqueness. Without diminishing the uniqueness of each situation, it is possible to consider a few types of adults who live out the faith with different approaches:

- believing adults, who live their faith and want to get to know it better

- adults who, although they may have been baptized, have not been adequately formed or have not brought Christian initiation to completion, and can be referred to as *quasi-catechumens*

- baptized adults, who although they do not live out their faith on a regular basis, nonetheless seek out contact with the ecclesial community or particular times in life

- adults who come from other Christian confessions or from other religious experiences

- adults who return to the Catholic faith having had experiences in the new religious movements

- unbaptized adults who are candidates for the catechumenate properly so called (258)

The general task of catechesis with adults needs to be configured in reference to the different types of persons and religious experiences in question (258).

Create a Prototype

What if we offered adult faith formation tailored to the adult faith profiles using four categories of experiences, programs, activities, and resources?

- "Taste and see" experiences
- "Refresher" experiences
- "Growing" experiences
- "Going deeper" experiences

Design: Scripture Study focused on the new Lectionary Cycle

Introduction to the Gospel

- Online two-part video-based introduction using videos from The Bible Project (**https://bibleproject.com**)
- Podcasts and audio programming on the Gospel

Exploration of the Gospel

(FOUR SESSIONS)

Four-week speaker series: Overview of Gospel, Teachings of Jesus, Ministry of Jesus, and Passion-Resurrection

- Gathered format at church (morning and evening sessions)
- Streamed live online
- Recorded for viewing on YouTube
- Offered as a four-session small-group format with videos and study guide

Growing and Going Deeper through Bible Study

Six-session Bible study of the Gospel

- At church with morning and evening sessions for small groups
- Small groups in homes or other setting
- Online small groups using Zoom
- On-your-own learning

Going Deeper through an Online Gospel Course

Eight-session online course for on-your-own learning or small-group learning

Curated On-Your-Own Resources

- Bible websites
- Online Bible apps
- Books and video programs

Families with Young Children

Target Audience
Families with young children (age 0–5)

Design Challenge
How to guide parents in forming the faith of their children from Baptism through start of school?

Connect to the **Directory for Catechesis**
The five tasks of catechesis promote an integral Christian life and holistic formation: knowledge of the faith, understanding and experience of liturgical celebrations, Christian formation of the moral conscience, educating for prayer and in prayer, and developing belonging to the Church and living its mission.

The catechumenal model and process includes:

- A first proclamation of the Gospel (kerygma)
- A comprehensive introduction to the Christian life
- Liturgies, rituals, and symbols that engage the heart and the senses
- A community of faith and support
- Apprenticeship and mentoring in faith
- Engagement in the mission of the Church and service to the world
- Formation that fosters conversion of heart and mind in a new way of life
- Ever-deeper formation in faith and the life of the community (mystagogy)

Create a Prototype
What if we created a catechumenal process and experiences for new parents and families with young children from Baptism to age 5–6?

Three Pathways through "Remote" Preparation for Baptism

1. For parents who have not been active in their faith life and practice: provide a first proclamation of the Gospel (kerygma) and then an introduction to the Christian life.

2. For parents who need a refresher: provide an introduction to the Christian life.

3. For parents who are growing in their faith: provide an exploration of the areas of the Christian life where they need growth.

"Immediate" Preparation for All Parents

- Catechesis on the sacrament to be celebrated: theology, rituals, and symbols
- Engagement with a community of faith and support—other parents or families and the intergenerational faith community
- Mentoring by members of the faith community

Celebration of the Sacrament

Continued Growth and Accompaniment (Mystagogy): Seven Elements of Faith Forming

- Specially curated collection of developmentally appropriate faith practices and activities for the growing family, delivered online and in print at six-month intervals: Bible stories, prayers, rituals, values formation, celebrating milestones, and more
- Celebrating the Church year seasons
- Practical resources for raising children: webinars, online resources, mentoring
- Just for Parents continuing formation in faith: webinars, online resources, mentoring
- Online support group for parents
- Gatherings at church for parents and children (quarterly)

Conclusion

"No one sews a piece of unshrunk cloth on an old cloak; otherwise, the patch pulls away from it, the new from the old, and a worse tear is made. And no one puts new wine into old wineskins; otherwise, the wine will burst the skins, and the wine is lost, and so are the skins; but one puts new wine into fresh wineskins." (MARK 2:21-23, NRSV CATHOLIC EDITION)

We believe this is a new moment for catechesis in the Catholic Church in the U.S. It is a time to put new wine into fresh wineskins. The models and approaches that have served us well in the past were never designed to address the significant challenges of the present time.

The *Directory for Catechesis* offers us fresh wine—a robust and holistic vision of catechesis for all ages and generations. It is up to us to create new wineskins—new models, approaches, and practices that embody the vision of the *Directory* and address the lives of our people today.

The title of our book—*Guided by the* Directory for Catechesis: *Transforming the Vision and Practice of Parish Catechesis*—embodies our hope for the Church. We believe with the *Directory* as our guide we can develop holistic, effective, innovative, and lifelong catechesis for all ages that speaks to the new context in which we live. It is up to us to make the vision and practices of the *Directory* come alive in our parish communities. As you create lifelong catechesis in your parish community, return often to the ideas contained in this book to assist you.

We believe that catechesis can form, renew, and revitalize the faith life of the whole parish community. It can contribute toward building a thriving parish community that becomes a learning community that lives its mission in the world. When a parish embraces lifelong formation in faith as essential to its mission and makes a commitment to create and sustain catechesis with families and all ages, the culture of the parish is strengthened and the faith of individuals flourishes.

We pray that you and your parish community will create fresh wineskins for the new vision of catechesis the Church offers us today.

Practice Resources Online at ncclcatholic.org

We have produced Practice Resources to assist you in applying the insights and practices in the book. You can download them from **ncclcatholic.org/guided-by-the-directory**. All of the Practice Resources are reproducible for use within your parish or ministry setting.

PRACTICE RESOURCE #1
A Guide to Creating the Purpose and Goals for Catechesis

PRACTICE RESOURCE #2
Assessment: Applying the Directory for Catechesis to Parish Life

PRACTICE RESOURCE #3
A Guide for Applying the Eight Practices from the Directory to Parish Catechesis

PRACTICE RESOURCE #4
Programming Approaches for Catechesis

PRACTICE RESOURCE #5
Assessment: Using Contemporary Methods for Catechesis

PRACTICE RESOURCE #6
Using Digital Methods in Catechesis

PRACTICE RESOURCE #7
Forming Faith with Families

PRACTICE RESOURCE #8
Parish Family Faith Formation Assessment

PRACTICE RESOURCE #9
What's Your Parish's Approach to Families?

**Practice Resource #10
Models of Family Catechesis**

PRACTICE RESOURCE #11
Practices for Forming Faith with Children

PRACTICE RESOURCE #12
Practices for Forming Faith with Adolescents

PRACTICE RESOURCE #13
Characteristics of the Seasons of Adulthood

PRACTICE RESOURCE #14
Learning Strategies for the Generations of Adulthood

PRACTICE RESOURCE #15
Designing Programming Using the Catechumenal Model and Process

PRACTICE RESOURCE #16
Practices for Forming Faith Intergenerationally

PRACTICE RESOURCE #17
Intergenerational Learning Design Worksheet

PRACTICE RESOURCE #18
Guide for Designing New Catechetical Initiatives

PRACTICE RESOURCE #19
Tools for Understanding Your Audience

Study the *Catechism of the Catholic Church* in 12 Convenient Booklets

Growing Faith

BY **BILL HUEBSCH**

Updated for today's multi-faceted parish, *Growing Faith* is pastoral, easy to use, and especially easy to facilitate.

Our Catholic faith is rooted in the deepest desires of the human heart: to know God and be with God, to know each other and be with each other. *Growing Faith* is designed to support this journey of faith and, when used from the first booklet to the last, it provides a systematic and comprehensive presentation of the Catholic faith.

God Is Always Near ▪ 857512

God Speaks with Us as Friends ▪ 857529

God Is the Source of Wisdom and Love ▪ 857536

Jesus Reveals God to Us 857543

Jesus Teaches Us to Practice Self-Giving Love ▪ 857550

Jesus Calls Us as Ambassadors ▪ 857567

We Are the People of God 857574

We Are the Body of Christ 857581

We Are a People of Mercy 857598

The Mystery of the Church 857604

The Mystery of Prayer ▪ 857611

The Mystery of the Sacraments ▪ 857628

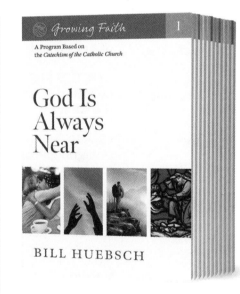

$2.95 EACH
Bulk pricing available as low as $1.95 each

Complete sets of all 12 booklets available as low as $16.95

All booklets are 24 pages and 5½" X 8½".

FREE LEADER'S GUIDE
AVAILABLE ONLINE

Suggestions for Use

☐ Parish Wide or Personal Use

☐ Adult Formation Groups, Middle-Aged and Senior Adults

☐ Families Who Have Children in Catechetical Programs

☐ Catechumens and Candidates in the RCIA Process

☐ Youth Groups, High School Faith Formation Groups, and Confirmation Programs

☐ Young Adults and Campus Ministry

☐ Intergenerational Catechetical Gatherings

☐ Households of Faith within the Parish

Whether you explore this study in groups or as individuals, you will find the beauty and deep meaning of our faith expressed in down-to-earth language written by best-selling author Bill Huebsch.

TO ORDER CALL **1-800-321-0411**
OR VISIT **23RDPUBLICATIONS.COM**

TWENTY-THIRD PUBLICATIONS